TWO TACTICS OF SOCIAL-DEMOCRACY
IN THE DEMOCRATIC REVOLUTION

TWO TACTICS

Of Social-Democracy
in the
Democratic Revolution

By V. I. LENIN

NEW YORK
INTERNATIONAL PUBLISHERS

INTRODUCTORY NOTE

THE present book was written in June and July, 1905, immediately after the Third Congress of the Russian Social-Democratic Labour Party, which was attended only by the Bolsheviks, and the Conference of the Mensheviks at Geneva.

In the resolutions of the Third Congress and of the Geneva Conference a fundamental disagreement was revealed, as Lenin put it, on "the estimation of the whole of the bourgeois revolution from the point of view of the tasks of the proletariat." During the first stage of the split with the Mensheviks, revealed at the Second Party Congress in London in 1903, the struggle had raged mainly around the question of the type of Party organisation to be set up (see Lenin's summation of this phase in his "One Step Forward, Two Steps Back," *Selected Works*, Vol. II). In his *Two Tactics of Social-Democracy in the Democratic Revolution*, Lenin compared the resolutions passed at the Bolshevik Congress and the Menshevik Conference and systematically elucidated the fundamental disagreements on the question of *tactics*, which arose out of differing conceptions of the character and driving forces of the bourgeois-democratic revolution in Russia, of the rôle of the proletariat and the prospects of the revolution.

As in his other writings in 1905, Lenin brings to the forefront the questions connected with a provisional government as the government of the revolutionary-democratic dictatorship of the proletariat and the peasantry and the problem of the armed uprising by which this dictatorship was to be achieved. He reveals the basic content of the position adopted by the Mensheviks in the 1905 Revolution—their tagging at the tail of the liberal bourgeoisie and their subordination of the interests of the proletariat to the interests of the bourgeoisie. The theories and practice of the Mensheviks, Lenin shows, were the Russian variety of revisionism and opportunism which at that time were already seriously sapping the strength of the Socialist Parties in Western Europe.

In his discussion of the revolutionary-democratic dictatorship of the proletariat and the peasantry, Lenin depicts the path of transition from the bourgeois-democratic to the proletarian revolution.

Two Tactics is a full elucidation of the policy followed by the Bolsheviks in the Revolution of 1905-1907, which Lenin later called the "dress rehearsal" of the Revolution of 1917.

To help the reader understand Lenin's numerous references to the events and personages of the period and his historical comparisons explanatory notes have been supplied by the editors which are to be found in the back of the book.

CONTENTS

PREFACE

In time of revolution it is very difficult to keep abreast of events, for they provide an astonishing amount of new material for the evaluation of the tactical slogans of revolutionary parties. The present pamphlet was written before the Odessa events. * We have already pointed out in *Proletary* ** (No. 9—"Revolution Teaches") that these events have forced even those Social-Democrats who created the "uprising-process" theory, and who rejected propaganda for a revolutionary provisional government, virtually to pass over, or to begin to pass over, to the side of their opponents.[2] Revolution undoubtedly teaches with a rapidity and thoroughness which appear incredible in peaceful epochs of political development. And what is of special importance, it not only teaches the leaders, but the masses as well.

There is not the slightest doubt that revolution will teach Social-Democracy to the working masses in Russia. Revolution will confirm the programme and tactics of Social-Democracy in actual practice, after demonstrating the true nature of the various social classes, the bourgeois essence of our democracy, and the real aspirations of the peasantry, which is revolutionary in a bourgeois-democratic sense and harbours not the idea of "socialisation," but that of a new class struggle between the peasant bourgeoisie and the village proletariat. The old illusions of the old Narodniks [3] so obviously reflected, for instance, in the draft programme of the Socialist-Revolutionary Party,[4] in their attitude towards the question of the development of capitalism in Russia, the question of the democratic character of our "society," and towards the question of the importance of a complete victory of the peasant rebellion—all these illusions will be mercilessly and finally blown to the winds by the revolution. It will give the various classes their first political baptism. These classes will emerge from the revolution with definite political features and reveal themselves, not only in the programmes

* This refers to the mutiny on the armoured cruiser *Potemkin*.[1] (Author's note to the 1908 edition.—*Ed.*)

** *Proletarian.* See footnote on p 27.—*Ed.*

9

and in the tactical slogans of their ideologists, but also in the open political action of the masses.

Undoubtedly, revolution will teach us and will also teach the masses of the people. But the question that now confronts a fighting political party is whether we shall be able to teach any lessons to the revolution; whether we shall be able to make use of our correct Social-Democratic doctrine, of our bond with the only consistently revolutionary class, the proletariat, in order to put a proletarian imprint on the revolution, in order to carry the revolution to real, decisive victory, in deeds and not in words, in order to paralyse the instability, half-heartedness, and treachery of the democratic bourgeoisie.

We must direct all our efforts to the achievement of this aim. And its achievement depends, on the one hand, on the correctness of our estimate of the political position, on the correctness of our tactical slogans and, on the other hand, on the extent to which these slogans are supported by real fighting forces of the masses of the workers. All the usual, regular current work of all organisations and groups of our Party, the work of propaganda, agitation and organisation, is directed towards strengthening and extending the ties with the masses. This work is always necessary and there can never be too much of it in time of revolution. At such a time the working class instinctively rushes into open revolutionary action, and we must know how correctly to define the tasks of this action, and then to spread a knowledge and understanding of these tasks as widely as possible. We must not forget that the pessimism now prevailing about our ties with the masses is very frequently a screen for bourgeois ideas on the role of the proletariat in the revolution. Undoubtedly, we still have a great deal to do to educate and organise the working class, but the crux of the matter now is: what is the main political centre of gravity of this work of education and organisation? Is it the trade unions and legal societies, or the armed insurrection and the creation of a revolutionary army and a revolutionary government? Both serve to educate and organise the working class. Both are necessary, of course. But the whole question now, in the present revolution, reduces itself to the following: what is the centre of gravity of the work of educating and organising the working class—the former or the latter?

The issue of the revolution depends on whether the working class will play the part of auxiliary to the bourgeoisie which is powerful in its onslaught against the autocracy, but impotent politically; or the part of leader of the people's revolution. The class conscious representatives of the bourgeoisie are perfectly well aware of this. That is precisely why *Osvobozhdeniye* * is praising Akimovism, "Economism" ** in Social-Democracy, which is *now* placing the trade unions and the legal societies in the forefront. That is why Mr. Struve welcomes (*Osvobozhdeniye*, No. 72) the trend of principles of Akimovism in the new *Iskra*.[5] That is why he comes down so heavily upon the hated revolutionary narrowness of the decisions of the Third Congress of the Russian Social-Democratic Labour Party.

It is particularly important at the present time for Social-Democracy to advance correct tactical slogans in order to guide the masses. There is nothing more dangerous in time of revolution than underestimating the importance of tactical slogans that are consistent in principle. *Iskra*, for instance, in No. 104, passes virtually to the side of its opponents in the Social-Democratic movement, and yet at the same time refers in disparaging tones to the significance of slogans and tactical decisions which are in advance of the times, which indicate the path along which the movement is progressing, with many failures, errors, etc.[6] On the other hand, the working out of correct tactical decisions is of immense importance for the Party, which desires to lead the proletariat in the spirit of the consistent principles of Marxism, and not merely to drag at the tail of events. In the resolutions of the Third Congress of the Russian Social-Democratic Labour Party and of the Conference of the section of the Party *** that seceded, we see the most pre-

---

* *Emancipation*, published by P. Struve in Stuttgart in 1902-1905, organ of the moderate liberals who belonged to the Emancipation League.—*Ed.*

** Akimovism, from the name of Akimov, the *nom de plume* of Makhnovets, one of the editors of *Rabocheye Dyelo* [*Worker's Cause*], a leading exponent of opportunism and Economism. The latter was a tendency within Russian Social-Democracy advocating that the workers restrict their activities to economic struggles and abstain from politics, leaving this field to the bourgeois liberals. For a full discussion of Economism see V. I. Lenin, *What Is To Be Done*, Little Lenin Library, Vol. 4, or *Collected Works, The Iskra Period*, Book II.—*Ed.*

*** The Third Congress of the Russian Social-Democratic Labour Party (held in London in May 1905) was attended only by Bolsheviks, while at the Geneva Conference held at the same time only Mensheviks participated. In the present pamphlet the latter are frequently referred to as new *Iskra*-ists, because while continuing to publish *Iskra* they declared, through their then adherent Trotsky, that there is a gulf between the old and the new *Iskra*. (Author's note to the 1908 edition.—*Ed.*)

cise, the most thought-out, the most complete expressions of tactical views, not those casually expressed by individual publicists, but those accepted by the responsible representatives of the Social-Democratic proletariat. Our Party stands in front of all the others, for it possesses a definite programme, accepted by all. It must set the example for all other parties also by strict adherence to its own tactical resolutions in contradistinction to the opportunism of the democratic bourgeoisie of *Osvobozhdeniye* and the revolutionary phrases of the Socialist-Revolutionaries, who only during the revolution suddenly bethought themselves of coming forward with a "draft" programme and of attending for the first time to the question as to whether what they are witnessing is a bourgeois revolution or not.

That is why we think that the most urgent task that confronts revolutionary Social-Democracy is carefully to study the tactical resolutions of the Third Congress of the Russian Social-Democratic Labour Party and of the Conference, to define what deviations have been made from the principles of Marxism and to have a clear grasp of the concrete tasks that confront the Social-Democratic proletariat in a democratic revolution. The present pamphlet is devoted to this task. The verification of our tactics from the standpoint of the principles of Marxism and of the lessons of the revolution is also necessary for those who really desire to prepare the ground for unity of tactics as a foundation for the future, complete unification of the whole Russian Social-Democratic Labour Party, and not to confine themselves to mere words of admonition.

N. Lenin.

July 1905.

I

An Urgent Political Question

THE question that stands in the forefront at the present time of revolution is that of the convocation of a constituent assembly. Opinions differ as to how this question is to be solved. Three political tendencies are to be observed. The tsar's government admits the necessity of assembling representatives of the people, but under no circumstances does it desire this assembly to be a national and constituent assembly. It seems willing to agree, if we are to believe the newspaper reports of the work of the Bulygin Commission,[7] to an advisory assembly, to be elected without freedom to carry on agitation and under an electoral system based on a high property qualification or on a narrow class system. The revolutionary proletariat, in so far as it is guided by Social-Democracy, demands the complete transfer of power to the constituent assembly, and for this purpose strives to obtain not only universal suffrage and complete freedom to conduct agitation, but also the immediate overthrow of the tsarist government and its replacement by a provisional revolutionary government. Finally, the liberal bourgeoisie, expressing its wishes through the leaders of the so-called "Constitutional-Democratic Party,"[8] does not demand the overthrow of the tsarist government, nor does it advance the slogan of a provisional government, or insist on real guarantees that the elections will be free and fair—that the assembly of representatives shall really be a national assembly and really a constituent assembly. As a matter of fact, the liberal bourgeoisie, which represents the only serious social support of the *Osvobozhdeniye* group, is striving to bring about as peaceful a compromise as possible between the tsar and the revolutionary people, a compromise, moreover, that would give the maximum of power to the bourgeoisie and the minimum to the revolutionary people, the proletariat and the peasantry.

Such is the political situation at the present time. Such are the three main political tendencies, corresponding to the three main social forces of contemporary Russia. On more than one occasion we have shown (in *Proletary*, Nos. 3, 4, 5) how the *Osvobozhdeniye*-ists cover up their half-hearted, or, to express ourselves more directly and simply, their treacherous, policy towards the revolution by sham democratic phrases. Let us now consider how the Social-Democrats estimate the tasks of the moment. The two resolutions passed quite recently by the Third Congress of the Russian Social-Democratic Labour Party and the "Conference" of the seceded section of the Party provide excellent material for this purpose. The question as to which of these resolutions more correctly appraises the political situation and more correctly defines the tactics of the revolutionary proletariat is of immense importance, and every Social-Democrat who is anxious to fulfil his duties as a propagandist, agitator and organiser intelligently must study this question very carefully and leave all irrelevant matters entirely aside.

By Party tactics we mean the political behaviour of the Party, or the character, tendency or methods of its political activity. Tactical resolutions are adopted by Party congresses for the purpose of determining exactly what the political behaviour of the Party as a whole should be in regard to new tasks, or in regard to a new political situation. The revolution that has started in Russia has created precisely such a new situation, *i.e.*, a complete, decisive and open rupture between the overwhelming majority of the people and the tsarist government. The new question is: what practical methods are to be adopted to convene a genuinely national and genuinely constituent assembly (the question of such an assembly was settled by Social-Democracy in theory long ago, before any other party, in its Party programme). If the people have parted company with the government, and the masses have realised the necessity of setting up a new order, then the party which made it its object to overthrow the government is of necessity forced to consider what it is to put in place of the old government about to be overthrown. A *new* question arises about the provisional revolutionary government. In order to give a complete answer to this question the party of the class conscious proletariat must make clear: (1) the *significance* of a provisional revolutionary government in the present revolution and in the struggle waged by the proletariat in general; (2) its *attitude* to the provisional revolutionary government; (3) the precise conditions on which *Social-Democracy will join* this government; (4) the conditions of pressure to be brought to bear on this government *from below, i.e.*, in the event of the Social-Democrats

14

not participating in it. Only after all these questions are cleared up, will the political behaviour of the Party in this connection be one of principle, definite and firm.

Let us now consider how the resolution of the Third Congress of the Russian Social-Democratic Labour Party answers these questions. The following is the full text of the resolution:

RESOLUTION ON THE PROVISIONAL REVOLUTIONARY GOVERNMENT

Taking into consideration,

1. That both the immediate interests of the proletariat and the interests of its struggle for the final aims of socialism demand the widest possible measure of political freedom and, consequently, that the autocratic form of government be replaced by a democratic republic;

2. That the setting up of a democratic republic in Russia is possible only as a result of a victorious uprising of the people, whose organ of government will be the provisional revolutionary government, the only body capable of securing complete freedom for electoral agitation and of convening, on the basis of universal, equal, direct suffrage and secret ballot, a constituent assembly that will really express the will of the people;

3. That under the present social and economic order this democratic revolution in Russia will not weaken, but strengthen, the domination of the bourgeoisie, which will inevitably, at a certain moment, by all manner of means, strive to filch from the Russian proletariat as many of the gains of the revolutionary period as possible;

The Third Congress of the Russian Social-Democratic Labour Party resolves that:

(a) it is necessary to make the working class understand concretely the most probable course of the revolution and the necessity of the appearance at a certain moment of a provisional revolutionary government, from whom the proletariat will demand the satisfaction of all the immediate political and economic demands contained in our programme (the minimum programme);

(b) subject to the relation of forces, and other factors which cannot be exactly determined beforehand, representatives of our Party may participate in the provisional revolutionary government for the purpose of ruthlessly combating all counter-revolutionary attempts and of defending the independent interests of the working class;

(c) a necessary condition for such participation is that the Party shall maintain strict control over its representatives and that the independence of Social-Democracy, which is striving for a complete socialist revolution and therefore is irreconcilably hostile to all the bourgeois parties, shall be strictly maintained;

(d) irrespective of whether the participation of Social-Democracy in the provisional revolutionary government will prove possible or not, it is necessary to propagate among the broadest possible strata of the proletariat the necessity of permanent pressure being brought to bear upon the provisional government by the armed proletariat, led by Social-Democracy, for the purpose of defending, consolidating and extending the gains of the revolution.

II

What Does the Resolution of the Third Congress of the Russian Social-Democratic Labour Party on the Provisional Revolutionary Government Teach Us?

THE resolution of the Third Congress of the Russian Social-Democratic Labour Party, as is seen from its title, wholly and exclusively deals with the question of the provisional revolutionary government. Hence, it includes the question as to whether Social-Democrats may participate in a provisional revolutionary government. On the other hand, it deals only with the provisional revolutionary government and with nothing else; consequently, it does not include, for example, the question of the "conquest of power" in general, etc. Did the Congress act properly in eliminating this and similar questions? Undoubtedly it was right in doing so, because the present political situation of Russia does not raise such questions as immediate issues. On the contrary, the issue raised by the entire people at the present time is the overthrow of autocracy and the convocation of a constituent assembly. Party congresses must take up and decide issues which are of serious political importance because of the conditions prevailing at the time and because of the objective course of social development and not those questions which in season or out of season are touched upon by this or that publicist.

What is the significance of the provisional revolutionary government in the present revolution, and in the general struggle of the proletariat? The resolution of the Congress explains this by pointing out from the outset the necessity of the "widest possible measure of political liberty," both from the standpoint of the immediate interests of the proletariat and from the standpoint of the "final aims of socialism." And full political liberty requires that the tsarist autocracy be replaced by a democratic republic, as is already recognised by our Party programme. It is necessary to stress the slogan of a democratic republic in the resolution of the Congress both from the point of view of logic and of principles; for the proletariat, being the foremost champion of democracy, is striving precisely for complete freedom. Moreover it is all the more necessary to stress this at the present time because precisely at this moment the monarchists, the so-called "Constitutional-Democratic," or *Osvobozhdeniye* Party in this country, is coming out under the

16

flag of "democracy." In order to set up a republic, an assembly of people's representatives is absolutely necessary. Moreover, such an assembly must necessarily be a national (on the basis of universal, equal and direct suffrage and secret ballot) and constituent assembly. This too is recognised in the resolution of the Congress, further on. But the resolution does not confine itself to this. In order to set up a new order "that will really express the will of the people" it is not enough to call the elected assembly a constituent assembly. That assembly must have power and force to "constitute." Taking this into consideration, the resolution of the Congress does not confine itself to the formal slogan of a "constituent assembly," but adds the material conditions which alone will enable that assembly to fulfil its tasks. The statement of the conditions which will enable an assembly which is a constituent assembly in name to become a constituent assembly in fact is urgently necessary, for, as we have pointed out more than once, the liberal bourgeoisie, as represented by the Constitutional-Monarchist Party, is deliberately distorting the slogan of a national constituent assembly and reducing it to an empty phrase.

The resolution of the Congress states that *only* a provisional revolutionary government can secure full freedom for the election campaign and convene an assembly that will really express the will of the people, moreover, an assembly that will be the organ of a victorious people's uprising. Is this postulate correct? Those who take it into their heads to refute it will have to assert that the tsarist government will not side with the reaction, that it is capable of being neutral during the elections, that it will see to it that the will of the people is really expressed. Such assertions are so absurd that no one would venture to advance them openly; but it is precisely the adherents of *Osvobozhdeniye* who are secretly smuggling them into our midst under the cover of a liberal flag. The constituent assembly must be convened by someone; someone must guarantee the freedom and fairness of the elections; someone must invest such an assembly with full power and force. Only a revolutionary government, which is the organ of the uprising, can in all sincerity desire this and be capable of doing everything to achieve this. The tsarist government will inevitably oppose it. A liberal government which comes to terms with the tsar, and which does not rely entirely on the people's uprising, cannot sincerely desire this and could not achieve it even if it desired it most sincerely. Therefore, the resolu-

17

tion of the Congress gives the only correct and entirely consistent democratic slogan.

However, the evaluation of the importance of the provisional revolutionary government would be incomplete and erroneous if the class nature of the democratic revolution were lost sight of. The resolution therefore adds that the revolution will strengthen the domination of the bourgeoisie. This is inevitable under the present, *i.e.*, capitalist, social and economic system. And the result of the strengthening of the domination of the bourgeoisie over the proletariat after it has secured some political liberty, however slight, must inevitably be a desperate struggle for power between them, must lead to desperate attempts on the part of the bourgeoisie "to filch from the proletariat the gains of the revolutionary period." The proletariat which is fighting for democracy in front and at the head of all must therefore be ever mindful of the new antagonisms and the new struggles which are inherent in bourgeois democracy.

Thus, the part of the resolution which we have just reviewed fully appreciates the importance of the provisional revolutionary government in connection with the struggle for freedom and for the republic, in connection with the constituent assembly and in connection with the democratic revolution, which clears the ground for a new class struggle.

The next question is, what should be the attitude of the proletariat in general towards the provisional revolutionary government? The Congress resolution answers this first of all by directly advising the Party to spread among the working class the conviction that a provisional revolutionary government is necessary. The working class must perceive this necessity. While the "democratic" bourgeoisie leaves the question of the overthrow of the tsarist government in the shade, we must push it to the fore and insist on the necessity of a provisional revolutionary government. More than that, we must outline a programme of action of such a government, which should conform to the objective conditions of the historic period we are living in and to the aims of proletarian democracy. This programme is the *entire* minimum programme [9] of our Party, the programme of the immediate political and economic reforms which, on the one hand, are quite attainable in the existing social and economic relationships and, on the other hand, are necessary in order to be able to take the next step forward in the direction of achieving socialism.

The resolution thus fully explains the nature and the aims of the provisional revolutionary government. By its origin and fundamental nature such a government must be the organ of the people's rebellion. Its formal purpose must be to serve as an instrument for the convocation of a national constituent assembly. Its activities must be directed towards the achievement of the minimum programme of proletarian democracy, which is the only programme capable of securing the protection of the interests of the people which has risen against the autocracy.

It might be argued that the provisional government, owing to the fact that it is provisional, could not carry out a positive programme which had not yet received the approval of the whole of the people. Such an argument would be sheer sophistry, such as is advanced by reactionaries and "autocratists." To abstain from carrying out a positive programme is tantamount to tolerating the existence of the feudal regime of the putrid autocracy. Only a government of traitors to the cause of the revolution could tolerate such a regime, and certainly not a government which is the organ of the people's rebellion. It would be mockery for anyone to propose that we should refrain from exercising freedom of assembly pending the confirmation of such freedom by the constituent assembly, on the plea that the constituent assembly might not confirm freedom of assembly! Similarly, it would be mockery to object to the immediate carrying out of the minimum programme by the provisional revolutionary government.

Finally, we wish to say that by making it the task of the provisional revolutionary government to achieve the minimum programme, the resolution thereby eliminates the absurd, semi-anarchist ideas that the maximum programme, the conquest of power for a socialist revolution, can be immediately achieved.[10] The present degree of economic development of Russia (an objective condition) and the degree of class consciousness and organisation of the broad masses of the proletariat (a subjective condition indissolubly connected with the objective condition) make the immediate, complete emancipation of the working class impossible. Only the most ignorant people can ignore the bourgeois character of the present democratic revolution; only the most naive optimists can forget how little as yet the masses of the workers are informed of the aims of socialism and of the methods of achieving it. And we are all convinced that the emancipation of the workers can only be brought

19

about by the workers themselves; a socialist revolution is out of the question unless the masses become class-conscious, organised, trained and educated by open class struggle against the entire bourgeoisie. In answer to the anarchist objections to the effect that we are delaying the socialist revolution, we shall say: we are not delaying it, but are taking the first step in its direction, using the only means that are possible along the only right path, namely, the path of a democratic republic. Whoever wants to approach socialism by another path, other than political democracy, will inevitably arrive at absurd and reactionary conclusions in the economic and in the political sense. If any workers ask us at any given moment: why not carry out our maximum programme, we would answer by pointing out how much the masses of the democratically disposed people are still ignorant of socialism, how much class antagonisms are still undeveloped, how much the proletarians are still unorganised. Organise hundreds of thousands of workers all over Russia; enlist the sympathy of millions for our programme! Try to do this without confining yourselves to high-sounding but hollow anarchist phrases. You will see at once that in order to achieve this organisation, in order to spread socialist enlightenment, we must have democratic reforms on the widest possible scale.

Let us proceed further. Having explained the significance of the provisional revolutionary government and the attitude of the proletariat towards it, the following question arises: would we be right in participating in it (action from above) and, if so, under what conditions? What should be our action from below? The resolution supplies precise answers to both these questions. It definitely declares that in principle, it is *right* for Social-Democracy to participate in the provisional revolutionary government (during the epoch of a democratic revolution, an epoch of struggle for the republic). By this declaration we irrevocably dissociate ourselves from the anarchists who, in point of principle answer this question in the negative, and also from the *khvost*-ists * among the Social-Democrats (such as Martynov and the new *Iskra*-ists) who *tried to frighten* us with the prospect of a situation in which it might prove necessary for us to take part in such a government. By this declaration the Third Congress of the Russian Social-Democratic Labour Partly irrevocably rejected the idea expressed by the new *Iskra* that

* Dragging at the tail of the movement of the masses; from the Russian word *khvost,* meaning tail.—*Ed.*

the participation of Social-Democrats in the provisional revolutionary government is a variety of Millerandism,* that it is inadmissible in principle, because it thus gives its sanction to the bourgeois regime, etc.

But the question of whether it is admissible or not in principle does not, of course, solve the question of practical expediency. Under what conditions is this new form of struggle—the struggle "from above" as recognised by the Congress of the Party—expedient? It goes without saying that at the present time it is impossible to speak of concrete conditions, such as relation of forces, etc., and the resolution, naturally, does not define these conditions in advance. No sensible person would venture at the present time to prophesy anything on this subject. What we can and must do is to determine the nature and aim of our participation. This precisely is done by the resolution, which points out two aims of our participation: (1) to ruthlessly combat counter-revolutionary attempts, and (2) to defend the independent interests of the working class. At a time when the liberal bourgeoisie is beginning to talk freely about the psychology of reaction (see Mr. Struve's most edifying "Open Letter" [11] in *Osvobozhdeniye* No. 72), and is trying to frighten the revolutionary people into yielding to the autocracy—at such a time it is particularly appropriate for the party of the proletariat to call attention to the task of waging a real war against counter-revolution. In the final analysis, force alone can settle the great problems of political liberty and class struggle, and it is our business to prepare and organise this force and to use it actively, not only for defensive purposes, but also for the purpose of attack. The long reign of political reaction in Europe, which has lasted almost uninterruptedly since the days of the Paris Commune, has too greatly accustomed us to the idea that action can only proceed "from below," has accustomed us to seeing only defensive struggles. There can be no doubt that we have now entered a new epoch: a period of political upheavals and revolutions has been ushered in. In a period such as Russia is passing through at the present time, we cannot limit ourselves to the old set formulas. It is necessary to propagate the idea of action from above, to prepare for the most energetic, offen-

* A. Millerand was the first Socialist to join a bourgeois cabinet (1899-1902), where he sat with General Gallifet, the suppressor of the Paris Commune. He was expelled from the party in 1904, served in many Cabinets and was President of France in 1920-1924.—*Ed.*

sive actions, to study the conditions and forms of these actions. The Congress resolution lays special emphasis on two of these conditions: one refers to the formal side of the participation of Social-Democracy in the provisional revolutionary government (strict control of the Party over its representatives), the other—to the very nature of such participation (never for an instant to lose sight of the aim of bringing about a complete socialist revolution).

Having thus explained from all aspects the policy of the Party in action "from above"—this new, hitherto almost unprecedented method of struggle—the resolution then provides for the case when we shall not be able to act "from above." We must exercise pressure on the provisional revolutionary government from below in any case. In order to be able to exercise this pressure from below, the proletariat must be armed—for in a revolutionary situation things develop very quickly to the stage of civil war—and must be led by Social-Democracy. The object of its armed pressure is that of "defending, consolidating and extending the gains of the revolution," *i.e.*, those gains which from the standpoint of proletarian interests must consist of the achievement of the whole of our minimum programme.

This brings our brief analysis of the resolution of the Third Congress on the provisional revolutionary government to a close The reader will see that this resolution explains the importance of this new question, the attitude of the Party of the proletariat towards it, and the policy of the Party both in and out of the provisional revolutionary government.

Let us now consider the corresponding resolution of the "Conference."

III

What is a "Decisive Victory of the Revolution over Tsarism"?

THE resolution of the "Conference" deals with the question: *"The Conquest of Power and Participation in the Provisional Government."* * As we have pointed out already, there is a patent con-

---

* The full text of this resolution can be reconstructed by the reader from the quotations given on pp. 400, 403, 407, 431 and 433 of the present pamphlet. (Author's note to the 1908 edition. *Cf.* pp. 23, 28-29, 34, 65 and 69 in this volume.—*Ed.*)

fusion in the very manner in which the question is put. On the one hand the question is presented in a narrow sense; it deals only with our participation in the provisional government and not with the tasks of the Party in regard to the provisional revolutionary government in general. On the other hand, two totally heterogeneous questions are mixed up, *viz.*, the question of our participation in one of the stages of the *democratic* revolution and the question of the *socialist* revolution. Indeed, the "conquest of power" by Social-Democracy is precisely the socialist revolution, and it cannot be anything else if we use these words in their direct and usually accepted sense. If, however, we understand these words to mean the conquest of power, not for a socialist, but for a democratic revolution, then, of course, there is no sense in talking about participation in the provisional revolutionary government and the "conquest of power" *in general.* Obviously our "Conference-ists" were not clear in their own minds as to what they should talk about: about the democratic revolution or about the socialist revolution. Those who have followed the literature on this question know that it was Comrade Martynov, in his famous *Two Dictatorships,* who started this muddle: the new *Iskra*-ists are very reluctant to recall the manner in which this question was presented (before January 22 [9]) in that model tailist work. However, there can be no doubt that it exercised ideological influence on the Conference.

But let us leave the title of the resolution. Its contents reveal mistakes incomparably more profound and serious. Here is the first part:

A decisive victory of the revolution over tsarism may be marked either by the setting up of a provisional government, which emerges from a victorious people's uprising, or by the revolutionary initiative of this or that representative institution, which under the immediate pressure of the revolutionary people decides to set up a national constituent assembly.

Thus, we are told that a decisive victory of the revolution over tsarism may be achieved by a victorious uprising, and—a decision of a representative institution to establish a constituent assembly! Whatever does this mean? A decisive victory may be marked by a "decision" to set up a constituent assembly?? And such a "victory" is put side by side with the establishment of a provisional government "which emerges from the victorious people's uprising"!! The Conference failed to notice that a *victorious* people's uprising and the *setting up* of a provisional government would signify the victory of the revolution *in deeds,* whereas a "decision" to set up a constituent assembly would signify a victory of the revolution *in words* only.

The Conference of the Menshevik new *Iskra*-ists committed the same error that the liberals of *Osvobozhdeniye* are constantly committing. The *Osvobozhdeniye*-ists are prattling about a "constituent" assembly and they bashfully close their eyes to the fact that power and force remain in the hands of the tsar. They forget that in order to "constitute" one must possess the *force* to do so. The Conference also forgot that the "decision" of any sort of representatives whatsoever does not by a long way mean that the decision is carried out. The Conference also forgot that so long as power remains in the hands of the tsar, all decisions passed by any sort of representatives will remain empty and miserable prattle, as was the case with the "decisions" of the Frankfort Parliament, famous in the history of the German Revolution of 1848. [12] Marx, the representative of the revolutionary proletariat, in his *Die Neue Rheinische Zeitung,* castigated the Frankfort liberal *Osvobozhdeniye*-ists with merciless sarcasm precisely because they uttered fine words, adopted all sorts of democratic "decisions," "constituted" all kinds of liberties, while in reality they left power in the hands of the king and failed to organise an armed struggle against the armed forces at the disposal of the king. And while the Frankfort *Osvobozhdeniye*-ists were prattling—the king bided his time, consolidated his military forces, and the counter-revolution, relying on real force, utterly routed the democrats with all their beautiful "decisions."

The Conference put on a par with a decisive victory the very thing that lacks the essential condition of victory. How is it to be explained that Social-Democrats who recognise the republican programme of our Party committed that error? In order to understand this strange phenomenon we must turn to the resolution of the Third Congress on the seceded section of the Party. *

* This reads as follows: [13] "The Congress declares that since the time of the Party's fight against Economism, certain trends have survived in the Party which, in various degrees and respects, are akin to Economism and which betray a common tendency to belittle the importance of the element of consciousness in the proletarian struggle, and to subordinate it to the element of spontaneity. On questions of organisation, the representatives of these tendencies put forward, in theory, the principle of organisation-process which is out of harmony with methodical Party work, while in practice they deviate from Party discipline in very many cases and in other cases they preach the wide application of the elective principle to the least educated section of the Party, without

This resolution refers to the fact that various tendencies "akin to Economism" have survived in our Party. Our "Conference-ists" (it is not for nothing that they are under the ideological guidance of Martynov) talk of the revolution in exactly the same way as the Economists talked of the political struggle or the eight-hour day. The Economists at once resorted to the "stages theory": (1) struggle for rights, (2) political agitation, (3) political struggle; or, (1) a ten-hour day, (2) a nine-hour day, (3) an eight-hour day. The results of this "tactics-process" is sufficiently well known to all. Now we are invited to divide the revolution itself into distinct stages: (1) the tsar convenes a representative institution; (2) this representative institution "decides" under the pressure of the "people" to set up a constituent assembly; (3) . . . the Mensheviks have not yet agreed among themselves as to the third stage; they have forgotten that the revolutionary pressure of the people will encounter the counter-revolutionary pressure of tsarism and that, therefore, either such a "decision" will remain unfulfilled or else the matter will be settled after all by the victory or the defeat of the people's uprising. The resolution of the Conference is exactly as if the Economists were to argue as follows: a decisive victory of the workers may be marked either by the revolutionary introduction of the eight-hour day or by the grant of a ten-hour day and the "decision" to pass on to a nine-hour day. . . . The two arguments are exactly alike.

Perhaps someone will say that the authors of the resolution did not mean to place the victory of the uprising *on a par* with the "decision" of a representative institution convened by the tsar, that they only wanted to provide for Party tactics in either case. To this our answer would be: (1) the text of the resolution directly

taking into consideration the objective conditions of Russian life and so strive to *undermine* the only principle of Party ties that is now applicable. In tactical questions these trends manifest themselves in a tendency to narrow the scope of Party work, by declaring themselves opposed to completely independent Party tactics towards the liberal bourgeois parties, by opposing the possibility and desirability of our Party assuming the organising role in the people's uprising and by opposing the participation of our Party in a provisional democratic revolutionary government under any conditions whatsoever.

"The Congress invites all Party members to conduct an ideological struggle everywhere against such partial deviations from the principles of revolutionary Social-Democracy; at the same time it is of the opinion that persons who share such views to a more or less extent may participate in Party organisations provided they recognise Party Congresses and the Party rules and wholly submit to Party discipline." (Author's note to the 1908 edition.—*Ed.*)

and unambiguously describes the *decision* of a representative institution as "a decisive victory of the revolution over tsarism." Perhaps this is the result of careless wording, perhaps it could be corrected after consulting the minutes, but, so long as it is not corrected, there can only be one meaning in the present wording, and this meaning is entirely in keeping with the line of reasoning of *Osvobozhdeniye;* (2) the *Osvobozhdeniye* line of reasoning into which the authors of the resolution have fallen comes out in incomparably greater relief in other literary productions of the new *Iskra*-ists. For instance, in the organ of the Tiflis Committee, *Social-Democrat* (in the Georgian language; praised by *Iskra* in No. 100), the article, "The Zemsky Sobor * and Our Tactics," goes so far as to say that the "tactics" which make the Zemsky Sobor the centre of our activities" (about the convocation of which, we may add, nothing definite is known!) *"are more advantageous for us"* than the "tactics" of an armed uprising and of the setting up of a provisional revolutionary government. We shall refer to this article again further on. (3) No objection can be made to a preliminary discussion of what tactics the Party should adopt, either in the event of a victory of the revolution or in the event of its defeat, either in the event of a successful uprising, or in the event of the uprising failing to flare up into a serious force. Perhaps the tsarist government may succeed in convening a representative assembly for the purpose of coming to terms with the liberal bourgeoisie—the resolution of the Third Congress provides for that by directly referring to "hypocritical policy," "pseudo-democracy," "grotesque forms of people's representation similar to the so-called Zemsky Sobor." ** But the

* National Assembly—an assembly of notables, an advisory body convened from time to time by the tsars in the sixteenth and seventeenth centuries. Before 1905, this term was vaguely used to cover any kind of national assembly.—*Ed.*

** The following is the text of this resolution on the attitude to the tactics of the government on the eve of a revolution:

"Taking into consideration that the government, for the purpose of self-preservation during the present revolutionary period, while intensifying the usual repressions directed mainly against the class-conscious elements of the proletariat, at the same time (1) tries by means of concessions and promises of reforms politically to corrupt the working class and thereby divert it from the revolutionary struggle; (2) for the same purpose clothes its hypocritical policy of concessions in a pseudo-democratic cloak, beginning with invitations to the workers to elect their representatives to commissions and conferences and ending with creating grotesque forms of people's representation, similar to the so-called Zemsky Sobor; (3) organises the so-called Black Hundreds and rouses

point is that this is not the resolution on the provisional revolutionary government, for it has nothing to do with the provisional revolutionary government. This case puts the problem of the uprising,
and of the setting up of a provisional revolutionary government,
somewhat in the background; it modifies this problem, etc. The
point is not whether all kinds of combinations are possible, whether
there will be victory or defeat, whether events pursue a straight path
or circuitous paths; the point is that a Social-Democrat must not
confuse the minds of the workers in regard to the true revolutionary
path, that he must not, like *Osvobozhdeniye*, describe as a decisive
victory that which lacks the *fundamental* condition of victory. We
may not even obtain the eight-hour day at one stroke, but only after
following a long circuitous path; but what would you say of a man
who describes such impotence, such weakness of the proletariat as
prevents it from counteracting the delays, haggling, treachery and
reaction, as a victory for the workers? It is possible that the Russian revolution will result in a "constitutional abortion," as was
once stated in *Vperyod*, * but can this justify a Social-Democrat,
on the eve of a decisive struggle, in calling this abortion a "decisive
victory over tsarism"? If it comes to the worst, we may not get a
republic, and even the constitution we get will be a mere phantom,

against the revolution generally all the reactionary and ignorant elements of
the people, or those blinded by racial or religious hatred.
"The Third Congress resolves to call on all Party organisations:
"(a) While exposing the reactionary purpose of the government's concessions, to emphasize by propaganda and agitation, firstly, the fact that these
concessions were forced on the government and, secondly, that it is absolutely
impossible for the autocracy to grant reforms satisfactory to the proletariat;
"(b) While taking advantage of the election campaign, to explain to the
workers the real meaning of the government's measures and to prove the necessity for the proletariat having the constituent assembly convened in a revolutionary way on the basis of universal, equal and direct suffrage and secret
ballot;
"(c) To organise the proletariat for the immediate achievement by revolutionary means of the eight-hour day and of other urgent demands of the working class;
"(d) To organise armed resistance to the actions of the Black Hundreds and
generally of all reactionary elements led by the government." (Author's note
to the 1908 edition.—*Ed.*)
* The Geneva newspaper *Vperyod* began to appear in January 1905 as the
organ of the Bolshevik section of the Party. Eighteen issues appeared from
January to May. After May, by virtue of the decision of the Third Congress
of the Russian Social-Democratic Labour Party, *Proletary* was issued in place
of *Vperyod* as the central organ of the R.S.D.L.P. (This Congress took place
in London in May; the Mensheviks did not appear, and organised their own
"Conference" in Geneva.) (Author's note to the 1908 edition.—*Ed.*)

"*à la* Shipov," [14] but would it be pardonable for a Social-Democrat to gloss over our republican slogan?

It is true, the new *Iskra*-ists have not yet gone so far as to gloss it over. But the resolution in which they have simply *forgotten* to mention a word about the republic illustrates very clearly to what extent they have become divorced from the revolutionary spirit, to what extent lifeless moralising has blinded them to the burning problems of the moment! It is incredible, but it is a fact. All the slogans of Social-Democracy have been endorsed, repeated, explained and worked out in detail in the various resolutions of the Conference, even the election of shop stewards and delegates by the workers has not been forgotten—but in a resolution on the provisional revolutionary government they forgot to mention the republic. To talk of a "victory" of the people's uprising, of the establishment of a provisional government, and not to indicate what relation these "steps" and acts have to winning the republic—means writing a resolution not for the guidance of the proletarian struggle, but for the purpose of hobbling along at the tail of the proletarian movement.

To sum up: the first part of the resolution (1) has not at all explained the significance of the provisional revolutionary government from the standpoint of the struggle for a republic and the guarantees for a genuinely national and genuinely constituent assembly; (2) has simply confused the democratic consciousness of the proletariat by placing a state of affairs in which the fundamental condition of a real victory is lacking on a par with the decisive victory of the revolution over tsarism.

IV

The Liquidation of the Monarchist System and the Republic

Let us pass on to the next part of the resolution:

In either case such victory will inaugurate a new phase in the revolutionary epoch.

The task, which is spontaneously set before this new phase by the objective conditions of social development, is the final liquidation of the whole estate-monarchist regime, to be carried out in the process of a mutual struggle among the elements of politically emancipated bourgeois society for the realisation of their social interests and for the immediate possession of power.

Therefore, the provisional government that would undertake to carry out the tasks of this revolution, which by its historical nature is a bourgeois revolution, would not only have to push revolutionary development further forward in regulating the mutual struggle of the conflicting classes of the emancipated nation, but also to fight against those of its factors, which threaten the foundations of the capitalist regime.

This part represents an independent section of the resolution. Let us examine it. The root idea underlying the above-quoted arguments coincides with that stated in the third clause of the Congress resolution. But in comparing these parts of the two resolutions, the following radical difference becomes at once apparent. The Congress resolution describes the social and economic basis of the revolution in a few words, concentrates its attention on the sharply defined struggle of classes for definite gains and places the militant tasks of the proletariat in the forefront. The resolution of the Conference describes the social and economic basis of the revolution in a long-winded, nebulous and involved way, very vaguely mentions the struggle for definite gains, and leaves the militant tasks of the proletariat altogether in the shade. The resolution of the Conference speaks of the liquidation of the old regime in the process of a mutual struggle among the various elements of society. The Congress resolution states that we, the party of the proletariat, must carry out this liquidation, that real liquidation can be brought about only by the establishment of a democratic republic, that we must win such a republic, that we will fight for it and for complete liberty, not only against the autocracy, but also against the bourgeoisie, if it attempts (as it is bound to do) to filch our gains from us. The Congress resolution calls on a definite class to wage a struggle for a precisely defined, immediate aim. The resolution of the Conference, however, discourses on the mutual struggle of various forces. One resolution expresses the psychology of active struggle, the other expresses that of passive contemplation; one breathes the call for lively activity, the other is full of lifeless moralising. Both resolutions state that the present revolution is only our first step, which will be followed by another; but one resolution draws therefrom the conclusion that we must for that reason get over this first step as quickly as possible, leave it behind, win the republic, mercilessly crush counter-revolution and prepare the ground for the second step. The other resolution, on the other hand, oozes out, so to speak, in verbose descriptions of this first step and (excuse the vulgar expression) chews the cud over it. The resolution of the Congress takes the old and the eternally new ideas of Marxism (about the bourgeois nature of the democratic revolution) as a preface or as a first premise for the progressive tasks of the progressive class, which is fighting both for the democratic and for the socialist revolution. The resolution of the Conference does not get beyond the preface, chewing it over and over again and trying to be clever about it.

This is precisely the distinction which for a long time past has been dividing the Russian Marxists into two wings: the moralising and the fighting wings in the old days of "legal Marxism," [15] and the economic and political wings in the epoch of the early mass movement. From the correct premise of Marxism concerning the deep economic roots of the class struggle generally and of the political struggle in particular, the Economists drew the peculiar conclusion that we must turn our backs on the political struggle and retard its development, narrow its scope, and diminish its tasks. The political wing, on the contrary, drew a different conclusion from these very premises, namely, that the deeper the roots of our struggle are now, the wider, the bolder, the more resolutely and with greater initiative must we wage this struggle. We are now engaged in the same old controversy, but under different circumstances and in a modified form. From the premises that the democratic revolution is not a socialist one, that it is not "of interest" to the propertyless only, that it is deep-rooted in the inexorable needs and requirements of the *whole* of bourgeois society—from these premises we draw the conclusion that all the more boldly therefore must the advanced class present its democratic tasks, and formulate them in the sharpest and fullest manner, put forward the direct slogan of the republic, advocate the need for the provisional revolutionary government and the necessity of ruthlessly crushing the counter-revolution. Our opponents, the new *Iskra*-ists, however, draw from the very same premises the conclusion that democratic principles should not be carried to their logical conclusion, that the slogan of a republic may be omitted from the practical slogans, that we can refrain from advocating the need for a provisional revolutionary government, that a decision to convene the constituent assembly can also be called a decisive victory, that we need not advance the task of fighting the counter-revolution as our active task, but that we may submerge it instead in a nebulous (and as we shall presently see, wrongly formulated) reference to the "process of mutual struggle." This is not the language of political leaders, but of fossilised officials!

And the more closely we examine the various formulæ in the new *Iskra*-ist resolution, the clearer we perceive its aforementioned basic features. It speaks, for instance, of the "process of mutual struggle among the elements of politically emancipated bourgeois society." Bearing in mind the subject with which this resolution deals (the provisional revolutionary government) we are rather surprised and ask: if we are talking about the process of mutual struggle, how can we keep silent about the elements which are politically *subjugating* bourgeois society? Do the "Conference-ists" really imagine that because they have assumed that the revolution will be victorious these elements have already disappeared? Such an idea would be absurd generally, and would express the greatest political naïveté and political short-sightedness in particular. After the victory of the revolution over the counter-revolution, the latter will not disappear; on the contrary, it will inevitably start a fresh, a still more desperate struggle. As the purpose of our resolution was to analyse the tasks that will confront us after the victory of the revolution, we had to devote considerable attention to the tasks of repelling counter-revolutionary attacks (as is done in the resolution of the Congress), not to submerge these immediate current and vital political tasks of a fighting party in general discussions on what will happen *after* the present revolutionary epoch, what will happen when "a politically *emancipated* society" will have come into existence. Just as the Economists, by repeating the truism that politics are subordinated to economics, covered up their failure to understand current political tasks, so the new *Iskra*-ists, by repeating the truism that struggles will take place in politically *emancipated* society, cover up their failure to understand the current revolutionary tasks of the political *emancipation* of this society.

Take the expression "the final liquidation of the whole estate-monarchist regime." In plain language, the final liquidation of the monarchist regime means the establishment of a democratic republic. But good Martynov and his admirers think that this expression is far too simple and clear. They must necessarily "deepen" it and say something "cleverer." As a result, we get ridiculous and vain efforts to appear profound, on the one hand, and, on the other hand, we get a description instead of a slogan, a sort of melancholy looking backward instead of a stirring appeal to march forward. We get the impression, not of virile people, eager to fight for a republic

31

here and now, but of fossilised mummies who *sub specie æternitatis* *
consider the question from the standpoint of *plusquam perfectum.* **
    Let us proceed further:

> . . . the provisional government . . . would undertake to carry out the
> tasks . . . of the bourgeois revolution. . . .

Here it transpires at once that our "Conference-ists" have overlooked
a concrete question which now confronts the political leaders of the
proletariat. The concrete question of the provisional revolutionary
government faded from their field of vision before the question of
the future series of governments which will accomplish the tasks
of the bourgeois revolution in general. If you want to consider the
question "from the historical standpoint," the example of any European country will show you that it was precisely a series of governments, not by any means "provisional," that carried out the historical
tasks of the bourgeois revolution, that even the governments which
defeated the revolution were none the less forced to carry out the
historical tasks of that defeated revolution.[16] But that which is
called "provisional revolutionary government" is something altogether different from what you are referring to: that is the name
given to the government of the revolutionary epoch, which immediately takes the place of the overthrown government and which relies
on the support of the people in revolt, and not on representative
institutions emanating from the people. The provisional revolutionary government is the organ of the struggle for the immediate
victory of the revolution, for the immediate repulse of counter-
revolutionary attempts, and is not an organ which carries out the
historical tasks of a bourgeois revolution in general. Well, gentlemen, let us leave it to the future historians on the staff of a future
Russkaya Starina *** to determine precisely which tasks of the bourgeois revolution you and we, or this or that government, have
achieved—there will be time enough to do that in thirty years; now
we must put forward slogans and give practical instructions for
the struggle for a republic, and for rousing the proletariat to take
a most active part in this struggle.
    For these reasons, the last postulates in the part of the resolution
which we have quoted above are unsatisfactory. The expression that

---

* From the standpoint of eternity.—*Ed.*
** The remote past.—*Ed.*
*** *Russian Antiquity*, an historical monthly journal published in St. Peters-
burg between 1870 and 1918.—*Ed.*

the provisional government would have to "regulate" the mutual struggle among the conflicting classes is exceedingly bad, or at any rate awkwardly put; Marxists should not use such liberal *Osvobozh-deniye* formulæ, which lead one to believe that we can conceive of governments which, instead of serving as organs of the class struggle, serve as its "regulators." . . . The government would "have not only to push revolutionary development further forward . . . but also to fight against those of its factors, which threaten the foundations of the capitalist regime." Such a "factor" is precisely the very same proletariat in whose name the resolution is speaking. Instead of indicating precisely how the proletariat at the given moment should "push revolutionary development further forward" (push it further than the constitutional bourgeoisie would be prepared to go), instead of advising definite preparations for a struggle against the bourgeoisie when the latter turns against the gains of the revolution—instead of all this, we are offered a general description of the process, which does not say a word about the concrete tasks of *our* activity. The new *Iskra*-ist method of exposition reminds one of Marx's reference (in his famous "theses" on Feuerbach) * to the old materialism, which was alien to the ideas of dialectics. Marx said that the philosophers only *interpreted* the world in various ways, our task is to *change* it. The new *Iskra*-ists also can describe and explain the process of struggle which is taking place before their eyes tolerably well, but they are altogether incapable of giving a correct slogan for this struggle. They march well but lead badly, and they degrade the materialist conception of history by ignoring the active, leading and guiding role in history which can and must be played by parties which understand the material prerequisites of a revolution and which have placed themselves at the head of the advanced classes.

* See F. Engels, *Ludwig Feuerbach* (International Publishers), Appendix, p. 73.—*Ed.*

V

How Should "The Revolution Be Pushed Further Forward"?

We now quote the next section of the resolution:

> Under such conditions, Social-Democracy must, during the whole course of the revolution, strive to maintain a position which would best of all secure for it the possibility of pushing the revolution forward, and which would not tie the hands of Social-Democracy in its struggle against the inconsistent and self-seeking policy of the bourgeois parties and preserve it from being merged with bourgeois democracy.
>
> Therefore, Social-Democracy must not strive to seize or share power in the provisional government, but must remain the party of the extreme revolutionary opposition.

The advice to take up a position which best secures the possibility of pushing the revolution further forward is very much to our taste. We only wish that in addition to good advice they had given a direct indication as to how Social-Democracy should push the revolution further forward now, in the present political situation, in a period of discussions, assumptions, talk and schemes for convening the people's representatives. Can the revolution be pushed further forward now by one who fails to understand the danger of the *Osvobozhdeniye* theory of "compromise" between the people and the tsar, who calls a mere "decision" to convene a constituent assembly a victory, who does not make it his task to carry on active propaganda in favour of a provisional revolutionary government, or who leaves in the shade the slogan of a democratic republic? Such people actually *push the revolution backward*, because as far as *practical politics* are concerned, they have remained on the level of the position taken by *Osvobozhdeniye*. What is the use of recognising a programme which demands that the autocracy be replaced by a republic, when in the tactical resolution, which defines the real and immediate tasks of the Party at a revolutionary moment, the slogan of struggle for a republic is missing? It is precisely the *Osvobozhdeniye* position, the position of the constitutional bourgeoisie, that is now characterised by the fact that they regard the decision to convene a national constituent assembly as a decisive victory and prudently keep silent about a provisional revolutionary government and the republic! In order to push the revolution *further forward*, *i.e.*, further than it is being pushed by the monarchist bourgeoisie, it is necessary actively to advance, emphasise and push to the forefront the slogans which *eliminate* the "inconsistencies" of bourgeois democracy. At the present time there are *only two* such slogans: (1) the provisional revolutionary government, and (2) the republic, for the slogan of a national constituent assembly has been *accepted* by the monarchist bourgeoisie (see the programme of the *Osvobozhdeniye* League) and accepted precisely for the purpose of cheating the revolution, of preventing the complete victory of the revolution, and for the purpose of enabling the big bourgeoisie to strike a huckster's bargain with tsarism. And now we see that of the two slogans which alone are capable of pushing the revolution further forward, the Conference completely forgot the slogan of a republic, and put the slogan of a provisional revolutionary government on a par with the *Osvobozhdeniye* slogan of a national constituent assembly, and called both "a decisive victory of the revolution"!!!

Yes, such is the undoubted fact, which, we are sure, will serve as a landmark for the future historian of Russian Social-Democracy. The Conference of Social-Democrats held in May 1905 passed a resolution which contains fine words about the necessity of pushing forward the democratic revolution and which in fact pushes it backward, which in fact does not go beyond the democratic slogans of the monarchist bourgeoisie.

The new *Iskra*-ists are wont to reproach us for our alleged ignoring of the danger of the proletariat merging with bourgeois democracy.[17] We should like to see anyone venture to prove such an assertion on the basis of the text of the resolutions passed by the Third Congress of the Russian Social-Democratic Labour Party. Our reply to our opponents is: Social-Democracy, acting on the basis of bourgeois society, cannot take part in politics, unless in this or that instance it marches *side by side* with bourgeois democracy. But the difference between us in this respect is that we march side by side with the revolutionary and republican bourgeoisie without merging with it, whereas you march side by side with the *liberal and monarchist bourgeoisie,* also without merging with it. *That is how the matter stands.*

The tactical slogans you advanced in the name of the Conference *coincide* with the slogans of the "Constitutional-Democratic" Party, *i.e.,* the *party of the monarchist bourgeoisie,* and you do not even notice or understand this coincidence, and thus drag at the tail of the *Osvobozhdeniye*-ist.

The tactical slogans we advanced in the name of the Third Congress of the Russian Social-Democratic Labour Party coincide with

the slogans of the democratic-revolutionary and republican bourgeoisie. This bourgeoisie and petty bourgeoisie in Russia have not
yet combined into a big people's party. *

However, only one utterly ignorant of what is now taking place
in Russia can doubt the existence of the elements of such a party.
We propose to lead (in the event of the great Russian revolution
proceeding successfully), not only the proletariat which will be
organised by the Social-Democratic Party, but also the petty bourgeoisie which is capable of marching side by side with us.

The Conference in its resolution unconsciously *stoops* to the level
of the liberal and monarchist bourgeoisie. The Party Congress in
its resolution consciously *raises* to its own level those elements of
revolutionary democracy which are capable of waging a struggle,
and will not act as brokers.

Such elements are to be found most among the peasants. When
we classify the big social groups according to their political tendencies we can, without danger of serious error, identify revolutionary
and republican democracy with the masses of the peasants in the
same way and with the same reservations and conditions, of course,
as we can identify the working class with Social-Democracy. In
other words, we may formulate our conclusions also in the following
expressions: the Conference in its *national* ** *political* slogans in a
revolutionary situation unconsciously *stoops to the level of the
masses of the landlords.* The Party Congress in its national political
slogans *raises the peasant masses to the revolutionary level.* To
anyone who may accuse us of betraying partiality for paradoxes in
drawing such a conclusion we make the following challenge: let him
refute the postulate that if we are not strong enough to bring the
revolution to a successful conclusion, if the revolution results in a
"decisive victory" in the *Osvobozhdeniye* sense, *i.e.*, in the form of
a representative assembly convened by the tsar, which could be
called a constituent assembly only as a joke—then this will be a
revolution with a preponderance of the *landlord and big bourgeois*
element. On the other hand, if we are destined to live through a
really great revolution, if history prevents "an abortion" this time,

* The Socialist-Revolutionaries are more in the nature of a terrorist group of
intellectuals than the embryo of such a party, although objectively, the activities of that group reduce themselves precisely to fulfilling the tasks of the revolutionary and republican bourgeoisie.

** We are not referring here to the special peasant slogans which were
dealt with in special resolutions.[18]

if we are strong enough to carry the revolution to the end, to final victory, not in the *Osvobozhdeniye* or the new *Iskra* sense of the word, then it will be a revolution with a predominance of the peasant and proletarian elements.

Perhaps some will regard the admission of the possibility of such a predominance as the renunciation of the view regarding the bourgeois character of the coming revolution. This is quite possible considering the way this concept is misused in *Iskra*. Therefore it will be useful to deal with this point.

VI

WHENCE THE DANGER OF THE PROLETARIAT HAVING ITS HANDS TIED IN THE STRUGGLE AGAINST THE INCONSISTENT BOURGEOISIE?

MARXISTS are absolutely convinced of the bourgeois character of the Russian revolution. What does this mean? It means that the democratic changes in the political regime and the social and economic changes which have become necessary for Russia do not in themselves imply the undermining of capitalism, the undermining of bourgeois domination; on the contrary, they will, for the first time, properly clear the ground for a wide and rapid European, and not Asiatic, development of capitalism, they will, for the first time, make it possible for the bourgeoisie to rule as a class. The Socialist-Revolutionaries cannot grasp this idea, for they are ignorant of the rudiments of the laws of development of commodity and capitalist production; they fail to see that even the complete success of a peasants' uprising, even the redistribution of the whole of the land for the benefit of the peasants according to their desires ("the Black Redistribution" * or something of that kind), will not destroy capitalism, but on the contrary will give an impetus to its development and will hasten the class disintegration of the peasantry itself. The failure to grasp this truth makes the Socialist-Revolutionaries unconscious ideologists of the petty bourgeoisie. It is extremely important for Social-Democracy, both from the theoretical and the practical-political standpoint, to insist on this truth, for from it logically arises the necessity of the complete class independence of the party of the proletariat in the present "general democratic" movement.

* Black Redistribution—the division of the whole land among the peasants, the traditional demand of the peasants. *Cf.*, V. I. Lenin, "Marx on the American 'Black Redistribution,'" *Marx, Engels, Marxism*, pp. 123 *ff.—Ed.*

But it does not at all follow from this that the *democratic* revolution (bourgeois in its social and economic content) is not of *enormous* interest for the proletariat. It does not at all follow that the democratic revolution could not take place in a form advantageous mainly to the big capitalist, the financial magnate, the "enlightened" landlord, and in a form advantageous to the peasant and to the worker.

The new *Iskra*-ists are radically wrong in their interpretation of the sense and significance of the concept, bourgeois revolution. Their arguments constantly reveal the underlying idea that the bourgeois revolution is a revolution which can only be of advantage to the bourgeoisie. And yet nothing is further removed from the truth. The bourgeois revolution is a revolution which does not go beyond the limits of the bourgeois, *i.e.*, capitalist, social and economic system. The bourgeois revolution expresses the needs of capitalist development, and not only does it not destroy the foundations of capitalism, but, on the contrary, it widens and deepens them. This revolution therefore expresses the interests not only of the working class, but also the interests of the whole of the bourgeoisie. Since, under capitalism, the domination of the bourgeoisie over the working class is inevitable, we are entitled to say that the bourgeois revolution expresses not so much the interests of the proletariat as those of the bourgeoisie. But the idea that the bourgeois revolution does not express the interests of the proletariat is altogether absurd. This absurd idea reduces itself either to the old-fashioned Narodnik theory that the bourgeois revolution runs counter to the interests of the proletariat and that, therefore, bourgeois political liberty is of no use to us; or to anarchism, which rejects all participation of the proletariat in bourgeois politics, in the bourgeois revolution and in bourgeois parliamentarism. Theoretically, this idea ignores the elementary postulates of Marxism concerning the inevitability of capitalist development on the basis of commodity production. Marxism teaches that at a certain stage of its development a society that is based on commodity production, and having commercial intercourse with civilised capitalist nations, inevitably takes the road of capitalism itself. Marxism has irrevocably broken with all the nonsense talked by the Narodniks and the anarchists about Russia, for instance, being able to avoid capitalist development, jump out of capitalism, or skip over it, by some means other than the class strug-gle on the basis and within the limits of capitalism.

All these principles of Marxism have been proved and explained in minute detail in general and with regard to Russia in particular. It follows from these principles that the idea of seeking salvation for the working class in anything save the further development of capitalism is *reactionary*. In countries like Russia, the working class suffers not so much from capitalism as from the lack of capitalist development. The working class is therefore undoubtedly interested in the widest, freest and speediest development of capitalism. The removal of all the remnants of the old order which are hampering the wide, free and speedy development of capitalism is of *absolute advantage* to the working class. The bourgeois revolution is precisely such a revolution which most resolutely sweeps away the survivals of the past, the remnants of serfdom (which include not only autocracy but monarchy as well); it is a revolution which most fully guarantees the widest, freest and speediest development of capitalism.

Therefore, the *bourgeois* revolution is in the *highest degree advantageous to the proletariat*. The bourgeois revolution is *absolutely* necessary in the interests of the proletariat. The more complete, determined and consistent the bourgeois revolution is, the more secure will the proletarian struggle against the bourgeoisie and for socialism become. Such a conclusion may appear new, or strange, or even paradoxical only to those who are ignorant of the rudiments of scientific socialism. And from this conclusion, among other things, follows the postulate that, *in a certain sense*, the bourgeois revolution is more *advantageous* to the proletariat than it is to the bourgeoisie. This postulate is undoubtedly correct in the following sense: it is to the advantage of the bourgeoisie to rely on certain remnants of the past as against the proletariat, for instance, on a monarchy, a standing army, etc. It is to the advantage of the bourgeoisie if the bourgeois revolution does not too resolutely sweep away the remnants of the past, but leaves some, *i.e.*, if this revolution is not fully consistent, if it does not proceed to its logical conclusion and if it is not determined and ruthless. Social-Democrats often express this idea somewhat differently by stating that the bourgeoisie betrays itself, that the bourgeoisie betrays the cause of liberty, that the bourgeoisie is incapable of being consistently democratic. It is to the advantage of the bourgeoisie if the necessary bourgeois democratic changes take place more slowly, more gradually, more cautiously, with less determination, by means of reforms and not by means of revolution; if these changes spare the "venerable" institutions of feudalism (such as the monarchy); if these reforms develop as little as possible the revolutionary initiative, the initiative and the energy of the common people, *i.e.*, the peasantry, and especially the workers, for otherwise it will be easier for the workers, as the French say, "to pass the rifle from one shoulder to the other," *i.e.*, to turn the guns which the bourgeois revolution will place in their hands, the liberty which the revolution will bring, the democratic institutions which will spring up on the ground that will be cleared of feudalism, against the bourgeoisie.

On the other hand, it is more advantageous for the working class if the necessary bourgeois-democratic changes take place in the form of revolution and not reform; for the latter is the road of delay, procrastination, of painfully slow decomposition of the putrid parts of the national organism. It is the proletariat and the peasantry that suffer first and most of all from this putrefaction. The revolutionary way is one of quick amputation, least painful to the proletariat, the way of direct amputation of the decomposing parts, the way of fewest concessions to and least consideration for the monarchy and the disgusting, vile, contaminating institutions which correspond to it.

So it is not only because of the censorship or through fear that our bourgeois-liberal press deplores the possibility of a revolutionary way, is afraid of revolution, tries to frighten the tsar with the bogey of revolution, is taking steps to avoid revolution, displaying servility and humility for the sake of miserable reforms, as a basis of the reformist way. This standpoint is not only shared by *Russkiye Vyedomosty, Syn Otechestva, Nasha Zhizn* and *Nashi Dni*,[19] but also by the illegal, uncensored *Osvobozhdeniye*. The very position the bourgeoisie as a class occupies in capitalist society inevitably causes it to be inconsistent in the democratic revolution. The very position the proletariat as a class occupies compels it to be consistently democratic. The bourgeoisie looks behind, is afraid of democratic progress which threatens to strengthen the proletariat. The proletariat has nothing to lose but its chains, but by means of democracy it has the whole world to win. Therefore, the more consistent the bourgeois revolution is in its democratic reforms the less will it limit itself to those measures which are advantageous only to the bourgeoisie. The more consistent the bourgeois revolution is, the more does it guarantee the advantages which the proletariat and the peasantry will derive from a democratic revolution.

Marxism teaches the proletarian not to keep aloof from the bourgeois revolution, not to refuse to take part in it, not to allow the leadership of the revolution to be assumed by the bourgeoisie but, on the contrary, to take a most energetic part in it, to fight resolutely for consistent proletarian democracy, to fight to carry the revolution to its completion. We cannot jump out of the bourgeois-democratic boundaries of the Russian revolution, but we can enormously extend those boundaries, and within those boundaries we can and must fight for the interests of the proletariat, for its immediate needs and for the prerequisites for training its forces for the complete victory that is to come. There are different kinds of bourgeois democracy. The Monarchist-Zemstvo member,[20] who advocated an upper chamber,[21] who is "haggling" for universal suffrage and who in secret, *sub rosa*, is striking a bargain with tsarism for a restricted constitution, is a bourgeois-democrat. And the peasant who is carrying on an armed struggle against the landlords and the government officials and with a "naive republicanism" proposes to "kick out the tsar" * is also a bourgeois-democrat. The bourgeois-democratic regime varies in different countries—in Germany and in England, in Austria and in America or Switzerland. He would be a fine Marxist indeed, who in a democratic revolution failed to see the difference between the degrees of democracy, between the different nature of this or that form of it, and confined himself to "clever" quips about this being "a bourgeois revolution" after all, the fruits of a "bourgeois revolution."

Our new *Iskra*-ists are precisely such wiseacres, proud of their short-sightedness. It is they who confine themselves to disquisitions on the bourgeois character of the revolution, on the questions as to when and where one must be able to draw a distinction between republican-revolutionary and monarchist-liberal bourgeois democracy, not to mention the distinction between inconsistent bourgeois democracy and consistent proletarian democracy. They are satisfied —as if they had really become like the "man in the case" **—to converse dolefully about the "process of mutual struggle of the conflicting classes," when what is needed is to give a *democratic lead*

* See *Osvobozhdeniye*, No. 71, page 337, footnote 2.[22]
** A character in one of Chekov's stories typifying a person secluded from the world.—*Ed.*

41

in a real revolution, to emphasise the *progressive democratic* slogans as distinguished from the treacherous slogans of Messrs. Struve and Co., to state straightforwardly and trenchantly the immediate tasks of the actual revolutionary struggle of the proletariat and the peasantry, as distinguished from the liberal broker tactics of the landlords and manufacturers. At the present time the crux of the matter lies in the following, which you, gentlemen, have missed, *viz.*, whether our revolution will result in a real, great victory, or in a miserable bargain, whether it will go as far as the revolutionary-democratic dictatorship of the proletariat and the peasantry, or whether it will exhaust itself in a liberal constitution "*à la* Shipov."

It might appear at first sight that by raising this question we are deviating entirely from our theme. But this may appear so only at first sight. As a matter of fact it is precisely this question that contains the roots of the difference in principle which has already become marked between the Social-Democratic tactics of the Third Congress of the Russian Social-Democratic Labour Party and the tactics inaugurated by the Conference of the new *Iskra*-ists. The latter have now taken three instead of two steps backward; they have revived the mistakes of Economism in solving problems that are far more complex, more important and more vital to the workers' party, *viz.*, the problem of its tactics in time of revolution. That is why we must bestow all our attention on an analysis of the question we have raised.

The section of the new *Iskra*-ist resolution which we have quoted above gives an indication of the danger of Social-Democracy tying its hands in the struggle against the inconsistent policy of the bourgeoisie, the danger of its becoming merged with bourgeois democracy. The consciousness of this danger runs like a thread throughout the whole of the specifically new *Iskra* literature, it is the crux of the whole principle at issue in our Party split (since the time squabbles have altogether been eclipsed by the tendencies towards Economism). And without beating about the bush we admit that this danger really exists and that precisely now, when the Russian revolution is in full swing, this danger has become particularly serious. The very urgent and exceedingly responsible task of finding out *from which side* this danger actually threatens is imposed on all of us theoreticians or—as I should prefer to style myself—the publicists of Social-Democracy. For the source of our disagreement is not the dispute as to whether such a danger exists, but the dispute as to whether it is caused by the so-called tailism of the "minority" or the so-called revolutionism of the "majority." *

To obviate all misinterpretations and misunderstandings, let us first of all remark that the danger which we are referring to lies not in the subjective, but in the objective side of the question, not in the formal position which Social-Democracy will take in the struggle, but in the material issue of the present revolutionary struggle. The question is not whether this or that Social-Democratic group will want to merge with bourgeois democracy or whether they are conscious of the fact that they are about to be merged. Nobody suggests that. We do not suspect any Social-Democrat of harbouring such a desire, and this is not a question of desires. Nor is it a question as to whether this or that Social-Democratic group will preserve its formal identity and independence apart from bourgeois democracy throughout the whole course of the revolution. They may not only proclaim such "independence" but preserve it in form, and yet *it may happen* that their hands will none the less be tied in the struggle against the inconsistency of the bourgeoisie. The final political result of the revolution may be that, in spite of the formal "independence" of Social-Democracy, in spite of its complete organisational independence as a separate party, it will in fact no longer be independent, it will not be able to put the impress of its proletarian independence on the course of events, and will prove so weak that, on the whole and in the last analysis, its "merging" with bourgeois democracy will none the less become an accomplished historical fact.

This is the real danger. Now let us see from which side it is threatening: from the fact that Social-Democracy, as represented by the new *Iskra*, is deviating to the Right, as we believe, or from the fact that Social-Democracy, as represented by the "majority," *Vperyod*, etc., is deviating to the Left, as the new *Iskra*-ists believe.

The solution of this question, as we have stated, is determined by the objective combination of the action of various social forces. The nature of these forces is theoretically determined by the Marxian analysis of Russian life, and is being practically determined now by the open actions of groups and classes in the course of the revolution. And at present the whole theoretical analysis, made by the Marxists long before the present epoch, as well as all the practical

---

* Minority and majority refer to Mensheviks and Bolsheviks, respectively.—*Ed.*

43

observations of the development of revolutionary events, shows that from the standpoint of objective conditions a twofold course and outcome of the revolution in Russia is possible. The reform of the economic and political system in Russia in the direction of bourgeois democracy is inevitable and unavoidable. There is no power on earth that can prevent such a change. But from the combination of the action of the existing forces which are bringing about that transformation two alternative results, or two alternative forms of that transformation may be obtained. Either (1) it will result in a "decisive victory of the revolution over tsarism," or (2) its forces will be inadequate for a decisive victory and the matter will end in a deal between tsarism and the most "inconsistent" and most "selfish" elements of the bourgeoisie. All the infinite varieties of detail and combinations which no one is able to foresee on the whole reduce themselves to either the one or the other of these issues.

Let us now consider these issues, first, from the standpoint of their social significance and, secondly, from the standpoint of the position of Social-Democracy (its "merging" or its "tied hands") resulting from either of these issues.

What is a "decisive victory of the revolution over tsarism"? We have already seen that in using this expression the new *Iskra*-ists do not grasp even its immediate political significance. Still less do they seem to understand the class content of this concept. Surely we Marxists must not allow ourselves to be deluded by *words,* such as "revolution" or "the great Russian revolution," as many revolutionary democrats (of the type of Gapon [23]) do. We must be perfectly clear in our own minds as to what real social forces are opposed to "tsarism" (which is a real force, perfectly intelligible to all) and are capable of gaining a "decisive victory" over it. Such a force cannot be the big bourgeoisie, the landlords, the manufacturers, not "society" which follows the lead of the *Osvobozhdeniye*-ists. We see that these do not even want a decisive victory. We know that owing to their class position they are incapable of undertaking a decisive struggle against tsarism: they are too greatly handicapped by the shackles of private property, capital and land to venture a decisive struggle. Tsarism with its bureaucratic police and military forces is far too necessary for them in their struggle against the proletariat and the peasantry for them to strive for the destruction of tsarism. No, only the *people* can constitute a force capable of gaining "a decisive victory over tsarism," in other

44

words, the proletariat and the peasantry, if we take the main, big forces and distribute the rural and urban petty bourgeoisie (also falling under the category of "people") between both of the two forces. "A decisive victory of the revolution over tsarism" is *the revolutionary-democratic dictatorship of the proletariat and peasantry*. Our new *Iskra*-ists will never be able to escape from this conclusion, which *Vperyod* pointed out long ago. There is no one else who is capable of gaining a decisive victory over tsarism.

And such a victory will assume the form of a dictatorship, *i.e.*, it is inevitably bound to rely on military force, on the arming of the masses, on an uprising, and not on institutions established by "lawful" or "peaceful" means. It can only be a dictatorship, for the introduction of the reforms which are urgently and absolutely necessary for the proletariat and the peasantry will call forth the desperate resistance of the landlords, the big bourgeoisie and tsarism. Without a dictatorship it will be impossible to break down that resistance and to repel the counter-revolutionary attempts. But of course it will be a democratic, not a socialist dictatorship. It will not be able (without a series of intermediary stages of revolutionary development) to affect the foundations of capitalism. At best it may bring about a radical redistribution of the land to the advantage of the peasantry, establish consistent and full democracy including the republic, eliminate all the oppressive features of Asiatic bondage, not only of village but also of factory life, lay the foundation for thorough improvement in the position of the workers and raise their standard of living, and last but not least *—carry the revolutionary conflagration into Europe. Such a victory will by no means transform our bourgeois revolution into a socialist revolution; the democratic revolution will not extend beyond the scope of bourgeois social and economic relationships; nevertheless, the significance of such a victory for the future development of Russia and of the whole world will be immense. Nothing will raise the revolutionary energy of the world proletariat so much, nothing will shorten the path leading to its complete victory to such an extent, as this decisive victory of the revolution that has now started in Russia.

Whether that victory is probable or not is another question. We are not the least inclined to be unreasonably optimistic on this score, we do not for a moment forget the immense difficulties of

* "Last but not least" in English in the Russian text.—*Ed.*
45

this task, but since we are out to fight we must wish to win and must be able to indicate the proper path to victory. Tendencies capable of leading to such a victory undoubtedly exist. It is true that our Social-Democratic influence on the masses of the proletariat is as yet exceedingly inadequate; the revolutionary influence on the masses of the peasantry is altogether insignificant; the dispersion, backwardness and ignorance of the proletariat, and especially of the peasantry, are still enormous. But revolution consolidates and educates rapidly. Every step in the development of the revolution rouses the masses and attracts them with uncontrollable force precisely to the side of the revolutionary programme as the only programme that consistently and logically expresses their real, vital interests.

The law of mechanics is that an action is equal to its counteraction. In history also the destructive force of the revolution is to a considerable extent dependent on how strong and protracted was the suppression of the striving for liberty, and how deep the contradiction between the antediluvian "superstructure" and the living forces of the present epoch. And the international political situation is in many respects shaping itself in a way most advantageous for the Russian revolution. The uprising of the workers and peasants has already started; it is sporadic, spontaneous, weak, but it unquestionably and undoubtedly proves the existence of forces capable of waging a decisive struggle and of marching onward to decisive victory.

If these forces prove inadequate, tsarism will have time to strike a bargain which is being prepared from both sides, both by Messrs. Bulygin and by Messrs. Struve. Then the whole thing will end in a curtailed constitution, or even, if things come to the worst, in an apology for a constitution. This will also be a "bourgeois revolution" but it will be an abortion, a half-baked, mongrel revolution. Social-Democracy cherishes no illusions on that score, it knows the treacherous nature of the bourgeoisie, it will not lose heart or abandon its persistent, patient, sustained work of giving a class education to the proletariat even in the most uninspiring, humdrum days of bourgeois-constitutional "Shipov" bliss. Such an outcome would be more or less similar to the outcome of almost all the democratic revolutions in Europe during the nineteenth century, and if it occurred in Russia, our Party development would proceed along the thorny, hard, long, but familiar and beaten track.

The question now arises: in which of the two possible outcomes of the revolution will Social-Democracy find its hands actually tied in the fight against the inconsistent and selfish bourgeoisie, find itself actually "merged," or almost so, with bourgeois democracy?

Once this question is clearly put, there is no difficulty in answering it without a minute's hesitation.

If the bourgeoisie succeeds in frustrating the Russian revolution by coming to terms with tsarism, Social-Democracy will find its hands actually tied in the fight against the inconsistent bourgeoisie; Social-Democracy will find itself merged with "bourgeois democracy" in the sense that the proletariat will not succeed in putting its clear imprint on the revolution and will not succeed in settling accounts with tsarism, in the proletarian or, as Marx used to say, "in the plebeian" way.

If the revolution gains a decisive victory—then we shall settle accounts with tsarism in the Jacobin,[24] or, if you like, in the plebeian way. "The terror in France," wrote Marx in 1848 in the famous *Die Neue Rheinische Zeitung,* "was nothing else than a plebeian method of settling accounts with the enemies of the bourgeoisie: with absolutism, feudalism and philistinism." (See Marx, *Nachlass,* Mehring's edition, Vol. III, p. 211.*) Have those who, in a period of democratic revolution, try to frighten the Social-Democratic workers in Russia with the bogey of "Jacobinism" ever stopped to think of the significance of these words of Marx?

The Girondists of contemporary Russian Social-Democracy, *i.e.,* the new *Iskra*-ists, do not merge with the *Osvobozhdeniye*-ists but, owing to the nature of their slogans, practically drag at the tail of the latter. And the *Osvobozhdeniye*-ists, *i.e.,* the representatives of the liberal bourgeoisie, wish to settle accounts with the autocracy gently, as befits reformers, in a yielding manner, so as not to offend the aristocracy, the nobles, the court—cautiously, without breaking anything—kindly and politely, as befits gentlemen in kid gloves, similar to those Mr. Petrunkevich borrowed from a bashi-bazuk **

* Lenin quotes from Marx's article, "The Balance Sheet of the Prussian Revolution."—*Ed.*
** Bashi-bazuk is an irregular Turkish soldier; the word is used ironically to describe the chief of the Tsar's bodyguard who offered his own gloves to Petrunkevich, a leader of the Constitutional-Democratic Party, when, on entering the Tsar's reception hall in the palace, it was suddenly discovered that he was without gloves.—*Ed.*

to wear at a reception of the "representatives of the people" (?) held by Nicholas the Bloody. (See *Proletary*, No. 5.)

The Jacobins of contemporary Social-Democracy—the Bolsheviks, the *Vperyod*-ists, the Congress-ists, the *Proletary*-ists, [25] I don't know what to call them—wish by their slogans to raise the revolutionary and republican petty bourgeoisie, and especially the peasantry, to the level of the consistent democracy of the proletariat, which fully preserves its class individuality. They want the people, *i.e.*, the proletariat and the peasantry, to settle accounts with the monarchy and the aristocracy in the "plebeian way," by ruthlessly destroying the enemies of freedom, suppressing their resistance by force, making no concessions to the accursed heritage of serfdom, of Asiatic barbarism and of the shameful treatment of human beings.

This, of course, does not mean that we necessarily propose to imitate the Jacobins of 1793, to adopt their views, programme, slogans and methods of action. Nothing of the kind. Our programme is not an old one, it is a new one—the minimum programme of the Russian Social-Democratic Labour Party. We have a new slogan: the revolutionary-democratic dictatorship of the proletariat and the peasantry. We shall also have, if we live to see a real victory of the revolution, new methods of action, corresponding to the character and aims of the working class party that is striving for a complete socialist revolution. We only want to explain by our comparison that the representatives of the advanced class of the twentieth century, the proletariat, *i.e.*, the Social-Democrats, are subdivided into two wings (the opportunist and the revolutionary) similar to those into which the representatives of the advanced class of the eighteenth century, the bourgeoisie, were divided, *i.e.*, the Girondists and the Jacobins.

Only in the event of a complete victory of the democratic revolution will the proletariat have its hands free in the struggle against the inconsistent bourgeoisie, only in that case will it not become "merged" with bourgeois democracy, but will leave its proletarian or rather proletarian-peasant imprint on the whole revolution.

In a word, in order that it may not find itself with its hands tied in the struggle against the inconsistent bourgeois democracy, the proletariat must be sufficiently class conscious and strong to rouse the peasantry to revolutionary consciousness, to guide its attack, independently to bring about consistent proletarian democracy.

That is how matters stand with regard to the question of the danger of having our hands tied in the struggle against the inconsistent bourgeoisie—the question that was so unsatisfactorily settled by the new *Iskra*-ists. The bourgeoisie will always be inconsistent. There is nothing more naive and futile than attempts to set forth conditions and points, * which, if satisfied, would enable us to regard bourgeois democracy as a sincere friend of the people. Only the proletariat can be a consistent fighter for democracy. It may become a victorious fighter for democracy only if the peasant masses join it in its revolutionary struggle. If the proletariat is not strong enough for this, the bourgeoisie will put itself at the head of the democratic revolution and will impart to it the character of inconsistency and selfishness. Nothing but the revolutionary-democratic dictatorship of the proletariat and the peasantry can prevent this from happening.

Thus, we arrive at the undoubted conclusion that it is precisely the new *Iskra*-ist tactics, owing to their objective significance, that are *playing into the hands of bourgeois democracy*. Preaching organisational diffusiveness, going so far as to call for plebiscites, and the principle of compromise, the divorcement of Party literature from the Party, belittling the tasks of armed rebellion, confusing the national political slogans of the revolutionary proletariat with those of the monarchist bourgeoisie, the distortion of the prerequisites for a "decisive victory of the revolution over tsarism"—all this taken together constitutes exactly that policy of tailism in a revolutionary period which baffles the proletariat, disorganises it, confuses its mind and degrades the tactics of Social-Democracy, instead of pointing out the only way to victory and of rallying to the slogan of the proletariat all the revolutionary and republican elements of the people.

In order to confirm this conclusion, at which we arrived on the basis of our examination of the resolution, we will take up the same question from another angle. Let us see, first, how the simple and outspoken Menshevik in the Georgian *Social-Democrat* illustrates the new *Iskra* tactics. And secondly, let us see who indeed, in the present political situation, is using the new *Iskra* slogans.

* As was attempted by Starover in his resolution, annulled by the Third Congress, and as is attempted by the Conference in an equally unfortunate resolution. (The resolution referred to was adopted at the Second Party Congress in 1903.—*Ed.*)

VII

The Tactics of "Eliminating the Conservatives From the Government"

THE article in the organ of the Tiflis Menshevik "Committee" (*Social-Democrat*, No. 1) which we referred to above, is entitled *The Zemsky Sobor and Our Tactics*. Its author has not yet entirely forgotten our programme, he advances the slogan of the republic, but he discusses tactics in the following way:

> Two ways of achieving this goal (the republic) may be indicated: either to completely ignore the Zemsky Sobor convened by the government and defeat the government with armed force, form a revolutionary government and convene a constituent assembly. Or . . . to declare the Zemsky Sobor the centre of our activity, determine its composition and activities by armed force, and force it to declare itself a constituent assembly or else through it to convene a constituent assembly. These two tactics differ very sharply from each other. Let us see which of them is more advantageous for us.

That is how Russian new *Iskra*-ists state the ideas, which were subsequently incorporated in the resolution we have examined. Note that this was written before the battle of Tsusima,* before the Bulygin project saw the light of day. Even the liberals were losing patience and expressed their distrust in the pages of the legal press; but a social-democratic new *Iskra*-ist proved to be more credulous than the liberals. He declares that the Zemsky Sobor "is being convened," and trusts the tsar to such an extent that he proposes to make the as yet non-existing Zemsky Sobor (or perhaps "the State Duma" or "Advisory Legislative Assembly?") the centre of our activities. Being more outspoken and straightforward than the authors of the resolution passed by the Conference, our Tiflisian does not put the two tactics (which he expounds with inimitable naïveté) on a par with each other, but declares that the second is more "advantageous." Just listen:

> The first tactics. As you know the coming revolution will be a bourgeois revolution, *i.e.*, it will bring about such changes in the present regime in which (the changes) not only the proletariat, but the whole of bourgeois society is interested. All classes, including even the capitalists, are in opposition to the government. The fighting proletariat and the fighting bourgeoisie in a certain sense are marching together and jointly attacking the autocracy from different sides. The government is entirely isolated and lacks public sympathy. Therefore, it is very easy to destroy it. The whole of the Russian proletariat is not so class-conscious and organised as to be able to carry out the revolution by

---

* A naval battle in the Russo-Japanese war of 1904-05 in which the Russian fleet suffered defeat.—*Ed.*

itself. If it were able to do so it would bring about a proletarian (a socialist), not a bourgeois revolution. Therefore, it is in our interests that the government remain without allies, and that it shall not be able to divide the opposition and ally to itself the bourgeoisie and leave the proletariat isolated. . . .

Thus. it is in the interests of the proletariat that the tsar's government shall not be able to separate the bourgeoisie from the proletariat!

Was it by mistake that this Georgian organ assumed the name of *Social-Democrat* instead of *Osvobozhdeniye?* And note the peerless philosophy of a democratic revolution! Is it not obvious that this poor Tiflisian is hopelessly confused by the moralizing tailist interpretation of the concept: "bourgeois revolution"? He discusses the question of the possible isolation of the proletariat in a democratic revolution and forgets . . . forgets only a trifle . . . the peasantry! The only possible allies of the proletariat he knows and cherishes are the landlord Zemstvo councillors—he is not aware of the peasants. Imagine this taking place in the Caucasus! Were we not right when we said that by its method of argument the new *Iskra* was sinking to the level of the monarchist bourgeoisie instead of elevating the revolutionary peasantry to be its allies?

. . . Otherwise the defeat of the proletariat and the victory of the government are inevitable. This is precisely what autocracy is aiming at. Undoubtedly in its Zemsky Sobor it will attract to its side the representatives of the nobility, the Zemstvos, the cities, the universities and other bourgeois institutions. It will try to win them over by small concessions and thus reconcile them to itself. Strengthened in this way, it will direct all its blows against the working people, which will then be isolated. It is our duty to prevent such an unfortunate issue. But can we prevent it by the first method? Let us assume that we paid no attention to the Zemsky Sobor and started to prepare an uprising by ourselves and on a certain day appeared in the streets armed and ready for the fray. We would then have to face two enemies: the government and the Zemsky Sobor. While we were preparing they had time to come to terms, enter into an agreement with each other, work out a programme advantageous to themselves, and share power between them. Such tactics would be of direct advantage to the government and we must repudiate them in a most energetic fashion. . . .

Now this is frank! We must resolutely abandon the "tactics" of preparing an uprising, because the government will "meanwhile" come to terms with the bourgeoisie! Could anything be found in the old literature of the most inveterate "Economism" that was anywhere near so disgraceful to revolutionary social-democracy? That outbursts and uprisings of workers and peasants break out here and there is a fact. The Zemsky Sobor is a vague promise on the part of Bulygin. And the *Social-Democrat* in the city of

Tiflis decides: to renounce the tactics of preparing an uprising and wait for the Zemsky Sobor—the "centre of activity"—to be convened. . . .

. . . The second tactics, on the contrary, are to make the Zemsky Sobor subject to our control, to prevent it acting as it pleases and making an agreement with the government.*

We support the Zemsky Sobor in so far as it will fight autocracy; and we will fight it in those cases when it reconciles itself to autocracy. By energetic interference and force we shall cause a split among the deputies.** We will rally the radicals to our side, eliminate the Conservatives from the government and thus put the whole Zemsky Sobor on the revolutionary road. By such tactics the government will always remain isolated, the position will remain strong, and thereby the establishment of a democratic regime will be facilitated.

Well, well! Let anybody now say that we exaggerate the turn of the new *Iskra*-ists to the most vulgar likeness to Economism. This is positively like the famous powder for exterminating flies: you first catch the fly, then bestrew it with this powder, and the fly will die. To split the deputies of the Zemsky Sobor by *force*, to "eliminate the Conservatives from the government" . . . and the *whole Zemsky Sobor* will strike a *revolutionary path*. . . . No "Jacobin" armed uprising is necessary: all they have to do is gently, almost in a parliamentary way, "influence" the *members of the Zemsky Sobor*.

Poor Russia! It has been said about her that she always wears old-fashioned bonnets that have been discarded by Europe. We have not yet got a parliament, Bulygin has not yet even promised one; but we already have an abundance of parliamentary cretinism.[27]

. . . How should this interference take place? First of all we will demand that the Zemsky Sobor be convened by means of universal, equal, direct suffrage with secret ballot; simultaneously with the proclamation *** of this method of election, freedom to carry on an election campaign must be enacted also,**** *i.e.*, freedom of assembly, speech, press, the inviolability of the electors and the elected and the release of all political prisoners. The elections must be fixed as late as possible so that we may have enough time to inform and prepare the people, and since the drafting of the regulations for convening the Sobor has been entrusted to the Commission headed by Bulygin, the Minister of the Interior, we must bring pressure to bear also on this commission

* By what means can the Zemstvo-ists be deprived of their free will? Perhaps a special sort of litmus paper? [26]
** Heavens!—"Profound" tactics indeed! No forces are available to fight in the streets, but it is possible to "split" the deputies . . . by force. Listen, comrades from Tiflis, prevarication is permissible, but within limits. . . .
*** In *Iskra?*
**** By Nicholas?

and its members.* If the Bulygin Commission refuses to satisfy our demands **
and grants the suffrage only to those possessing property, then we must inter-
fere in these elections and, in a revolutionary way, force the electors to elect
progressive candidates and, in the Zemsky Sobor, to demand a constituent assembly. Finally, by all sorts of means: demonstrations, strikes and if need be,
an uprising, we must force the Zemsky Sobor to convene a constituent assembly
or declare itself to be such. The armed proletariat must constitute itself the
defenders of the constituent assembly, and both * * * will then march towards
a democratic republic.

Such are social-democratic tactics and they alone will secure us victory.

Let not the reader imagine that this incredible rubbish is only a
first literary attempt on the part of some irresponsible uninfluential
new *Iskra*-ist. It is not—it was written in the organ of an entire
committee of new *Iskra*-ists—the Tiflis Committee. More than that.
This rubbish has been *directly approved by Iskra* in whose hun-
dredth issue we find the following stated about the *Social-Democrat.*

*The first issue is edited in bright and competent manner. The experienced
hand of a capable editor-publicist is perceptible. . . . We can say for certain
that the newspaper will brilliantly fulfil the task it has set itself.*

Yes!—If that task is to clearly demonstrate to all and sundry the
complete, hopeless ideological demoralisation of *Iskra*-ism, it has
indeed been "brilliantly" carried out. No one could have expressed
the *Iskra*-ists' degradation to the level of liberal bourgeois opportunism in a "brighter, more talented and competent" manner.

VIII

The Tendencies of the *Osvobozhdeniye* and of the New *Iskra*

Now let us pass on to another spectacular confirmation of the
political significance of the new *Iskra* tendency.

In his remarkable, excellent, instructive article "How to Find
Oneself" (*Osvobozhdeniye*, No. 71) Mr. Struve wages war against
the "revolutionism according to programme" of our extreme parties.
Mr. Struve is particularly displeased with me.****

* So this is what is meant by the tactics of "eliminating the Conservatives
from the government"!

** But surely such a thing cannot happen if we follow these correct and
profound tactics!

*** The armed proletariat as well as the Conservatives "eliminated from the
government"?

**** "In comparison with the revolutionism of Mr. Lenin and his associates,
the revolutionism of the West-European Social-Democrats, of Bebel and even
Kautsky, is opportunism, but the foundations even of this diluted revolutionism
have already been undermined and washed away by history." A very fierce sally.

I, on the other hand, am very pleased with Mr. Struve: I could not wish for a better ally in the struggle against the reviving Economism of the new *Iskra*-ists and the complete lack of principles displayed by the Socialist-Revolutionaries. On some other occasion we shall relate how Mr. Struve and *Osvobozhdeniye* proved in a practical manner how reactionary are the "amendments" to Marxism, contained in the draft programme of the Socialist-Revolutionaries. But we have already related, and shall tell it again, now, how Mr. Struve rendered me a faithful, honest and real service * each time he approved of the new *Iskra*-ists in principle.

Mr. Struve's article contains a number of very interesting statements, to which we can refer here only in passing. He is about to "create Russian democracy, relying in this, not on the class struggle but on class collaboration" so that "the socially privileged intelli-

---

Mr. Struve, however, is wrong in thinking that he can put all the blame on me, just as if I were dead. I can make a challenge to Mr. Struve, which he will never be able to accept. When and where did I call the revolutionism of Bebel and Kautsky "opportunism"? Where and when did I claim that I was creating a special trend in international social-democracy *not identical* with the trend represented by Bebel and Kautsky? Where and when did differences arise between me and Bebel and Kautsky even to any degree approximating in point of seriousness the differences between Bebel and Kautsky, for instance, in Breslau on the agrarian question? [28] Let Mr. Struve try to answer these three questions.

And to our readers we will say: the liberal bourgeoisie *always and everywhere* uses the strategy of persuading its adherents in a given country to believe that the Social-Democrats of that country are the most unreasonable ones, whereas their comrades in the neighbouring country are "good boys." The German bourgeoisie has pointed *hundreds of times* to the "good boys," the French Socialists, as models for the Bebels and the Kautskys. The French bourgeoisie quite recently put up the "good boy" Bebel as a model for the French Socialists. This is an old trick, Mr. Struve! You will only catch children and ignoramuses with that bait. It is an incontrovertible fact that international revolutionary social-democracy is unanimous on all the important questions of programme and tactics.

* We would remind the reader that the article *What Should Not Be Done* (*Iskra*, No. 52) was hailed with acclamation by *Osvobozhdeniye* as a "significant turn" toward concessions to the opportunists. The theoretical principles of the new *Iskra* were specially approved of by *Osvobozhdeniye* in a note on the split among the Russian Social-Democrats. Commenting on Trotsky's pamphlet, *Our Political Tasks*, *Osvobozhdeniye* pointed out the similarity between the ideas of that author with what was formerly written and said by the contributors to *Rabocheye Dyelo*: Krichevsky, Martynov, Akimov (see the leaflet *An Obliging Liberal* published by *Vperyod*). Martynov's pamphlet on the two dictatorships was welcomed by *Osvobozhdeniye* (*cf.* note in *Vperyod*, No. 9). Finally the belated complaints of Starover about the old slogan of the old *Iskra*, "First separate and then unite," met with special sympathy on the part of *Osvobozhdeniye*.

gentsia" (something like the "cultural nobility" to which Mr. Struve bows with the grace of a genuinely fashionable . . . valet) may bring the weight of its "social position" (that of the money bag) to this "non-class" party. Mr. Struve expresses the desire to inform the youth that the "radical stereotyped formula about the bourgeoisie being frightened and betraying the proletariat and the cause of liberty is impracticable." (We welcome this desire from the bottom of our heart. Nothing would confirm the correctness of this Marxian "stereotyped formula" better than a war against it waged by Mr. Struve. Please, Mr. Struve, don't put off your magnificent plan!)

For the purposes of our subject it is important to note the *practical slogans* against which this politically sensitive representative of the Russian bourgeoisie, who is so susceptible to the slightest change in the weather, is fighting at the present time. First of all he is fighting against the slogan of republicanism. Mr. Struve is firmly convinced that that slogan is "incomprehensible and alien to the masses of the people." (He forgets to add: comprehensible but not advantageous to the bourgeoisie!) We should like to see what answer Mr. Struve would get from the workers in our circles and at our mass meetings! Or perhaps the workers are not the people? What about the peasants? They sometimes display what Struve calls "naive republicanism" (to "kick out the tsar") — but the liberal bourgeoisie believes that this naive republicanism will be succeeded, not by conscious republicanism, but by conscious monarchism! *Ca dépend,* Mr. Struve; that depends on circumstances. Tsarism and the bourgeoisie cannot but oppose a radical improvement in the conditions of the peasantry at the expense of the landlords, but the working class cannot but assist the peasantry in this respect.

Secondly, Mr. Struve assures us, that "in civil war the attacking party will always be in the wrong." This idea approaches very closely to the above-described tendencies of the new *Iskra.* We will not say, of course, that in civil war it is *always* an advantage to attack. No; sometimes defensive tactics are absolutely necessary *for a certain period.* But to advance a proposition like that advanced by Mr. Struve in relation to Russia of 1905 means precisely to display a fragment of the "radical, stereotyped formula" ("The bourgeoisie is frightened and is betraying the cause of liberty"). Whoever now refuses to attack autocracy and reaction, whoever is not preparing himself for such an attack, whoever does not preach it—takes in vain the name of adherent of the revolution.

Mr. Struve condemns the slogans: "conspiracy" * and "riot" (this "uprising in miniature"). Mr. Struve spurns both from the point of view of "approaching the masses." We should like to ask Mr. Struve whether he can point to any passage in, for instance, *What Is To Be Done?*—the work of an extreme revolutionary from his standpoint—which advocates rioting. As regards "conspiracy" is there really very much difference between Struve and ourselves? Are we not both working in an "illegal" press, which is being "secretly" smuggled into Russia and which serves the "secret" groups of the "Emancipation League ** " and of the Russian Social-Democratic Labour Party? Our workers' mass meetings are often held "in secret"—yes, we must confess to that sin. But what about the meetings of *Osvobozhdeniye?* Is there anything you can boast of, Mr. Struve, to the contemptible partisans of contemptible conspiracy?

It is true, very strict secrecy is required in supplying arms to the workers. In this connection Mr. Struve is more outspoken. Just listen:

As regards an armed uprising or a revolution in a technical sense, only mass propaganda in favour of a democratic programme can create the social and psychological conditions of an universal armed uprising. Thus even from the standpoint that the armed uprising is the *inevitable* consummation of the present struggle for emancipation—a standpoint I do not share—the permeation of the masses with the ideas of democratic reform is the basic, the most necessary task.

Mr. Struve tries to dodge the issue. He talks about the inevitability of the uprising, instead of saying that it is necessary for the victory of the revolution. The uprising—unprepared, spontaneous, sporadic—has already started. No one can guarantee that it will develop into a compact and united armed uprising of the people, for that depends on the state of the revolutionary forces (which can be fully estimated only in the course of the struggle itself), on the behaviour of the government and the bourgeoisie, and on a number of other circumstances, which it is impossible to estimate exactly.

* Literally in Russian: *konspiratsiya*, meaning underground, or secret methods of work.—*Ed.*

** The League for the Emancipation of Labor, formed in 1883 by early Russian Marxists headed by Plekhanov, was a forerunner of the Russian Social-Democratic Labor Party.—*Ed.*

It is of no use talking about inevitability in the sense of the absolute certainty of a concrete event, as Mr. Struve does in evading the issue. If one wants to be a partisan of the revolution, one must discuss whether the uprising is *necessary for the victory* of the revolution, whether it should be actively pushed forward, preached and whether energetic and immediate preparations should be made for it. Mr. Struve cannot fail to understand this difference: he does not, for instance, obscure the necessity for universal suffrage, which no democrat denies, by the question as to whether universal suffrage is inevitable in the course of the present revolution, which statesmen regard as debatable and not urgent. By dodging the question of the necessity of an uprising, Mr. Struve expresses the motives that most deeply underlie the political position of the liberal bourgeoisie. The bourgeoisie, in the first place, prefers to come to terms with the autocracy rather than to crush it. In the second place, the bourgeoisie in any case leaves the task of the armed struggle to the workers. Such is the *real* meaning of Mr. Struve's evasiveness. That is why he *shirks* the question of the necessity of an uprising and falls back on the question of its "social and psychological" conditions, of "preliminary propaganda." Just as the bourgeois prattlers in the Frankfort Parliament of 1848 spent their time in drawing up resolutions, declarations, decisions, in "mass propaganda" and in preparing "social and psychological conditions," when they should have been resisting the government by armed force, when the movement had "created the necessity" of an armed struggle, when mere verbal pressure (which is a hundred times necessary in the period of preparation) became vulgar, bourgeois inactivity and cowardice—so Mr. Struve evades the question of an uprising by screening himself with *phrases*. Mr. Struve clearly displays what many Social-Democrats stubbornly fail to see, namely, that a revolutionary period differs from ordinary, every-day preparatory historical moments precisely in the fact that the temper, the excitement, the convictions of the masses must and do reveal themselves in action.

Vulgar revolutionism fails to grasp that a word is also a deed. This rule is indisputable when applied to history *generally* or to those epochs in history when no open, political mass actions take place; and a *putsch* cannot serve as a substitute for such actions, nor artificially call them forth. The tailist revolutionaries fail to understand that once a revolutionary period has started, when the old "superstructure" has cracked from top to bottom, when open political action on the part of classes and masses who are creating a new superstructure for themselves, has become an accomplished fact, when civil war has started—that to confine oneself to "words" as of *old*, at such a time without issuing the *direct slogan*: pass to "deeds," to avoid deeds on the plea of "psychological conditions" and "propaganda," is altogether either spiritless, lifeless sophistry, or the betrayal of the revolution, treachery to it. The Frankfort prattlers of the democratic bourgeoisie are an unforgettable historic example of such a betrayal, or of such stupid sophistry.

Do you want an explanation of this difference between vulgar revolutionism and the tailism of the revolutionaries by an example in the history of the social-democratic movement in Russia? We shall give you one. Recall the years 1901 and 1902, which are so recent and which already seem to us to be a remote legend. Demonstrations had started. Vulgar revolutionism raised an outcry about the "assault" (*Rabocheye Dyelo*), "bloody leaflets" were issued (if I am not mistaken, of Berlin origin), attacks were made on "literary zealots" and on the idea of conducting agitation all over Russia by means of a newspaper being the fancy of armchair dreamers (*Nadezhdin*). The tailist revolutionaries at that time preached that "the economic struggle is the *best* means of political agitation." [29] What was the attitude of revolutionary social-democracy? It attacked both of these tendencies. It condemned *putschism* and outcries about storming, for it was, or should have been, obvious to all that the outbreak of open mass action was only a matter of days. It condemned tailism and *even* advanced the slogan of a national armed uprising, not in the sense of a direct appeal (Mr. Struve would not have discovered any appeals to "riots" in our utterances in those days), but in the sense of a *necessary* deduction, in the sense of "propaganda" (of which Mr. Struve has only now bethought himself—our respected Mr. Struve is always a few years behind the times), in the sense of preparing the very "social and psychological conditions" about which the representatives of the perplexed, bargaining bourgeoisie are now babbling "so sadly and inappropriately." In *those* days, propaganda and agitation, agitation and propaganda, were really put in the forefront by the objective conditions. In *those* days the publication of an all-Russian newspaper, the weekly publication of which was regarded as an ideal, could be proposed (and was proposed in

What is to be Done?) as the touchstone of the work of preparing for an uprising. In *those* days the slogans: mass agitation *instead* of immediate armed actions; the preparation of social and psychological conditions of an uprising *instead* of *putschism*—were the only correct slogans of revolutionary social-democracy. *Now* these slogans have been surpassed by events, the movement has proceeded in advance of them, they have become mere lumber, tatters only fit to cover up the hypocrisy of the *Osvobozhdeniye*-ists and the tailists of the new *Iskra!*

Or perhaps I am mistaken? Perhaps the revolution has not started yet? Perhaps the moment for open political action of the classes has not yet arrived? Since there is no civil war yet, perhaps criticism by weapons ought not yet to be the immediate, *necessary* and obligatory successor, heir, trustee and executor of the weapon of criticism?

Look around; stick your head out of your study window and look into the street; you will find an answer to these questions there. Has not the government itself started civil war by shooting down masses of peaceful and unarmed citizens? Are not armed Black Hundreds coming out as the "arguments" of the autocracy? Has not the bourgeoisie—even the bourgeoisie—become conscious of the need for a civil militia? Does not Mr. Struve himself, the ideally moderate and punctilious Mr. Struve, say (alas, he only says so in order to evade the point!) that the "open character of revolutionary actions" (that's the sort of fellows we are today!) "is now one of the most important conditions for educating the masses of the people"?

Those who have eyes to see can never have any doubt as to how the partisans of the revolution must now present the question of an armed uprising. Consider then the *three* presentations of this question as given in those organs of the free press which are at all capable of influencing the *masses*.

The first presentation. The resolution of the Third Congress of the Russian Social-Democratic Labour Party. * It is publicly

* The following is its complete text:
Taking into consideration,
1. That the proletariat, being, in virtue of its position, the most progressive and the only consistently revolutionary class, is thereby called upon to play a leading part in the general democratic revolutionary movement of Russia;
2. That this movement has now created the necessity of an armed uprising;
3. That the proletariat will inevitably take a most active part in this uprising, which participation will determine the fate of the revolution in Russia;

acknowledged and declared that the general, democratic, revolutionary movement *has already created the necessity* of an armed uprising. The organisation of the proletariat for an uprising has been put on the order of the day as one of the essential, principal and *necessary* tasks of the Party. *Most energetic* measures to arm the proletariat and to secure the possibility of the immediate guidance of the uprising are urged.

The second presentation. The article in *Osvobozhdeniye* in which the "leader of the Russian Constitutionalists" (the title given to Mr. Struve by such an influential organ of the European bourgeoisie as the *Frankfurter Zeitung*), or the leader of the Russian progressive bourgeoisie, expounds his principles. He does not share the opinion that the uprising is inevitable. Conspiracy and riots are the specific methods of unreasonable revolutionism. Republicanism is the method of the club. The armed uprising is really only a technical question, whereas "the fundamental, the most necessary thing," is mass propaganda and the preparation of the social and psychological conditions.

The third presentation. The resolution of the new *Iskra*-ist Conference. Our task is to prepare an uprising. An uprising according to plan is out of the question. Favourable conditions for an uprising are created by disrupting the government, by our agitation,

4. That the proletariat can play a leading role in this revolution only by being welded into a united independent political force under the banner of the Social-Democratic Labour Party which is to guide its struggle not only ideologically but practically;

5. That only by performing this role can the proletariat secure the most favourable conditions for the struggle for socialism against the propertied classes of bourgeois-democratic Russia.

The Third Congress of the Russian Social-Democratic Labour Party recognises that the task of organising the proletariat for an immediate struggle against autocracy, by means of an armed uprising, is one of the most important and urgent tasks of the Party in the present revolutionary moment.

Therefore the Congress imposes on all the Party organisations the duty of:

(a) Explaining to the proletariat by means of propaganda and agitation not only the political importance, but also the practical organisational side of the coming armed uprising;

(b) Explaining in that propaganda and agitation the role of mass political strikes, which may have great importance in the beginning and in the very course of the uprising;

(c) Adopting the most energetic measures to arm the proletariat and also to work out a plan of an armed uprising and of the immediate guidance of same, creating for that purpose, to the extent that this becomes necessary, special groups from among Party workers. (Author's note to the 1908 Edition.—*Ed.*)

by our organisation. Only then "can technical-military preparations acquire more or less serious importance."

Is that all? Yes, that is all. The new *Iskra*-ist leaders of the proletariat do not yet know whether an uprising has become necessary. They are not yet clear in their minds as to whether the task of organising the proletariat for an immediate struggle has become urgent. It is not necessary to call for the adoption of most energetic measures; it is far more important (in 1905, not in 1902) to explain in general outlines under what conditions these measures "may" acquire "more or less serious" importance. . . .

Do you see now, comrades of the new *Iskra*, where your turn towards Martynovism has landed you? Do you understand that your political philosophy has turned out to be a rehash of the *Osvobozhdeniye* philosophy?—and that (against your will and unconsciously) you have found yourselves at the tail of the monarchist bourgeoisie? Is it clear to you now, that by repeating stale truths and perfecting yourselves in sophistry you have lost sight of the fact that—in the unforgettable words of the unforgettable article by Peter Struve—"the open character of revolutionary *actions* is at the present time one of the most important prerequisites for the education of the masses of the people?"

IX

WHAT DOES BEING A PARTY OF EXTREME OPPOSITION IN TIME OF REVOLUTION MEAN?

LET us revert to the resolution on the provisional government. We have shown that the tactics of the new *Iskra*-ists do not push the revolution further forward—the aim they set themselves in their resolution—but retard it. We have shown that it is precisely these tactics that *tie the hands* of Social-Democracy in its struggle against the inconsistent bourgeoisie and do not prevent it from becoming merged with bourgeois democracy. Naturally, the wrong premises of the resolution lead to wrong conclusions: "Therefore Social-Democracy must not strive to seize or share power in the provisional government, but must remain a party of extreme revolutionary opposition." Consider the first half of this conclusion, which is part of a statement of aims. Do the new *Iskra*-ists set a decisive victory of the revolution over tsarism as the aim of the Social-Democratic activity? They do. They are not able to formulate correctly the conditions for a decisive victory, and they stumble on the *Osvobozh-deniye* formulation, but they do set themselves the above-mentioned aim. Further: do they connect the provisional government with an uprising? Yes, they do so directly, by stating that the provisional government "emerges from a victorious uprising of the people." Finally, do they set themselves the aim of leading the uprising? Like Mr. Struve, they do not admit that the uprising is necessary and urgent, but unlike him, they say that "Social-Democracy is striving to *subordinate* it" (the uprising) "to its influence and *leadership* and to use it in the interests of the working class."

Now, isn't this logical? We set ourselves the *aim of subordinating* the uprising of the proletarian as well as *non-proletarian* masses to our influence, our leadership, and to use it in our interests. Accordingly, we set ourselves the aim of leading, in the course of the proletarian uprising, the revolutionary bourgeoisie and the petty bourgeoisie (the "non-proletarian groups") *i.e.*, of "*sharing*" the leadership of the uprising between Social-Democracy and the revolutionary bourgeoisie. We set ourselves the aim of securing *victory* for the uprising, which should lead to the establishment of a provisional government ("emerging from a victorious uprising of the people"). *Therefore* . . . therefore we must not aim at seizing or sharing power in the provisional revolutionary government!!

Our friends cannot think logically even if they try. They vacillate between the standpoint of Mr. Struve, who dissociates himself from an uprising, and the standpoint of revolutionary Social-Democracy, which calls upon us to undertake this urgent task. They vacillate between anarchism, which on principle condemns participation in a provisional revolutionary government as treachery to the proletariat, and Marxism, which demands such participation on condition that Social-Democracy is the leading influence in the uprising. They have no independent position: neither that of Mr. Struve, who wants to come to terms with tsarism and therefore is compelled to resort to evasions and subterfuges on the question of the uprising, nor that of the anarchists, who condemn all actions from "above" and all participation in a bourgeois revolution. The new *Iskra*-ists confuse striking a bargain with tsarism with securing a victory over tsarism. They want to take part in the bourgeois revolution. They have advanced somewhat, compared with Martynov's *Two Dictatorships.*

They even consent to lead the uprising of the people—in order to renounce that leadership immediately after victory is won (or, perhaps, immediately before the victory?), *i.e., in order to renounce the fruits of victory* and to turn them over *entirely to the bourgeoisie.* This is what they call "using the uprising in the interests of the working class. . . ."

There is no need to dwell on this muddle any longer. It will be more useful to examine how this muddle *originated* in the formula which reads: "to remain a party of extreme revolutionary opposition."

This is one of the familiar postulates of international revolutionary Social-Democracy. It is a perfectly correct postulate. It has become a truism for all opponents of revisionism or opportunism in parliamentary countries. It has become a recognised weapon in the legitimate and necessary resistance to "parliamentary cretinism," Millerandism, Bernsteinism * and the Italian reformism of the Turati brand. Our good new *Iskra*-ists have learned this excellent postulate by heart and are zealously applying it . . . *quite inappropriately.* The categories of parliamentary struggle are introduced into resolutions written for conditions in which no parliament exists. The concept "opposition," which became the reflection and the expression of a political situation in which no one seriously speaks of an *uprising,* is senselessly transplanted to a situation in which an uprising has actually *begun* and in which all the supporters of the revolution are talking and thinking about the leadership in such an uprising. The desire to *"stick"* to old methods, *i.e.,* action only "from below," is expressed with pomp and circumstance *precisely at a time* when the revolution has confronted us with the necessity, in the event of the uprising being victorious, of acting *from above.*

Well, our new *Iskra*-ists are decidedly out of luck! Even when they formulate a correct Social-Democratic postulate they don't know how to apply it correctly. They failed to take into consideration the fact that in the period when the revolution is beginning, when parliaments do not exist, when there is civil war and when outbursts of rebellion take place, the concepts and terms of the parliamentary struggle are changed and transformed into their opposites. They failed to take into consideration the fact that, under

---

* Eduard Bernstein, a Social-Democrat, attempted to effect a revision of the principles of revolutionary Marxism along reformist lines. He remained a leader of the Second International up to his death in 1933.—*Ed.*

the circumstances referred to, amendments are moved by way of street demonstrations, interpellations are introduced in the form of aggressive action by armed citizens, opposition to the government is expressed by violently overthrowing the government.

Like the famous hero of our folklore * who always gave good advice just when it was most out of place, our admirers of Martynov repeat the lessons of peaceful parliamentarism just at the moment when, as they themselves admit, direct military operations are commencing. Anything funnier than this pompous emphasis of the slogan "extreme opposition" in a resolution which begins by drawing attention to the "decisive victory of the revolution" and to the "people's uprising" cannot be imagined! Just imagine, gentlemen, what representing the "extreme opposition" means in the epoch of rebellion. Does it mean exposing the government or deposing it? Does it mean voting against the government or defeating its armed forces in open battle? Does it mean refusing supplies to the Treasury or does it mean the revolutionary seizure of the Treasury in order to apply it to the needs of the uprising, the arming of workers and peasants, the convocation of the constituent assembly? Are you not beginning to understand, gentlemen, that the term "extreme opposition" expresses only negative actions—to expose, to vote against, to refuse? Why? Because this term applies only to parliamentary struggle and to a period when no one makes "decisive victory" the immediate object of the struggle. Are you not beginning to understand that in this respect things change radically from the moment the politically oppressed people opens its determined attack along the whole front to win victory in desperate battle?

The workers ask us: should they energetically set to work to start the rebellion? What is to be done to make the incipient uprising victorious? How to make use of victory? What programme can and should be applied when victory is achieved? The new *Iskra*-ists who are making Marxism more profound answer: you must remain a party of extreme revolutionary opposition. . . . Well, were we not right in calling these knights past masters in philistinism?

* Ivan the fool.—*Ed.*

X

THE "REVOLUTIONARY COMMUNES" AND THE REVOLUTIONARY-DEMOCRATIC DICTATORSHIP OF THE PROLETARIAT AND THE PEASANTRY

THE new *Iskra*-ist Conference did not stick to the anarchist position which the new *Iskra* has talked itself into (only from "below," not "from below and from above"). The absurdity of conceiving of rebellion and not conceiving the possibility of victory and participation in the provisional revolutionary government was too strikingly obvious. The resolution therefore introduced certain reservations and restrictions into the solution of the question proposed by Martynov and Martov. Let us consider these reservations as stated in the following section of the resolution:

> These tactics ["to remain a party of extreme revolutionary opposition"] do not, of course, in any way exclude the expediency of a partial, episodic seizure of power and the formation of revolutionary communes in this or that city, in this or that district, exclusively for the purpose of helping to extend the uprising and to disrupt the government.

That being the case, it means that in principle they conceive of action, not only from below, but also from above. It means the renunciation of the postulate laid down in L. Martov's well-known article in *Iskra* (No. 93), and the endorsement of *Vperyod* tactics, *i.e.*, not only "from below," but also "from above."

Further, the seizure of power (even if it is partial or episodic, etc.) obviously presupposes the participation not only of Social-Democracy and the proletariat alone. This logically follows from the fact that it is not only the proletariat that is interested, and is taking part in, the democratic revolution. This logically follows from the fact that the uprising is a "people's uprising," as is stated in the beginning of the resolution we are discussing, that "nonproletarian groups" (the words used in the Conference resolution on the uprising), *i.e.*, the bourgeoisie, also take part in it. Hence, the principle that socialist participation in the provisional revolutionary government jointly with the petty bourgeoisie is treachery to the working class *was thrown overboard by the Conference, i.e.*, the very thing *Vperyod* was trying for. "Treachery" does not cease to be treachery because the action by which it is committed is partial, episodic, local, etc. Hence, the principle that participation in the provisional revolutionary government should be placed on a par with vulgar Jaurèsism * *was thrown overboard* by the Conference, as *Vperyod* insisted. A government does not cease to be a government because its power extends to a single city and not to many cities, to a single region and not to many regions; nor is the fact that it is a government determined by what it is called. Thus, the Conference rejected the principles that the new *Iskra* tried to formulate on this question.

Let us now see whether the restrictions imposed by the Conference on the formation of revolutionary governments, which in principle is now accepted, and on participation in such governments, are reasonable. What the difference is between the attributes "episodic" and "provisional" we do not know. We are afraid that this foreign and "new" word is intended to cover up a lack of clear thinking. It *appears* more "profound"; in fact it is only more foggy and confused. What is the difference between the "expediency" of a partial "seizure of power" in a city or district, and participation in a provisional revolutionary government in a whole country? Do not "cities" include one like St. Petersburg, where the memorable events of January 22 (9) ** took place? Do not regions include the Caucasus, which is bigger than many a state? Will not the problems (which at one time troubled the new *Iskra*) of what to do with prisons, the police, the Treasury, etc., confront us the moment we "seize power" in a single city, let alone in a region? No one will deny, of course, that if we lack sufficient forces, if the success of the uprising is incomplete, or if the victory is indecisive, city and other provisional revolutionary governments may arise. But what has all this to do with it, gentlemen? Did you yourselves not refer in the beginning of the resolution to the "decisive victory of the revolution," to "a victorious uprising of the people"?? Since when have the Social-Democrats assumed the task of the anarchists: to disperse the attention and the aims of the proletariat, to direct its attention to the "partial" instead of to the general, single, whole and complete? While presupposing the "seizure of power" in a single city, you yourselves speak of "extending the uprising," *i.e.*, to another city—may we venture to think, to hope that you mean all cities? Your conclusions, gentlemen, are as flimsy and casual, as self-contradictory and intricate as your premises. The Third Congress

---

* The policy advocated by the French Socialist leader, Jean Jaurès, of Socialists participating in bourgeois governments.—*Ed.*
** "Bloody Sunday," 1905. See note 23.—*Ed.*

of the Russian Social-Democratic Labour Party gave an exhaustive and clear answer to the general question of the provisional revolutionary government. This answer also embraces all the partial provisional governments. The answer given by the Conference, however, by artificially and arbitrarily singling out a *part* of the question, only *dodges* (but unsuccessfully) the question as a whole and creates confusion.

What does the term "revolutionary communes" mean? Does it differ from the term "provisional revolutionary government," and if so, in what respect? The Conference-ists themselves do not know. Confusion of revolutionary thought leads them, as very often happens, to a *revolutionary phrase*. Yes, words like "revolutionary commune" in a resolution passed by representatives of Social-Democracy represent a revolutionary phrase and nothing more. Marx more than once condemned such phrasemongering when fascinating terms of the *obsolete past* were used to hide the tasks of the future. In such cases, a fascinating term that has played its part in history is transformed into meaningless, harmful tinsel, a child's rattle. We must make it unequivocally clear to the workers and to the whole of the people *why* we want to set up a provisional revolutionary government, and precisely *what reforms* we shall carry out if we exercise decisive influence on the government on the morrow of the victorious people's uprising which has already commenced. Such are the questions that confront political leaders.

The Third Congress of the Russian Social-Democratic Labour Party gave perfectly clear answers to these questions and drew up a complete programme of these reforms: the minimum programme of our Party. The word "commune" is not an answer at all; like the distant echo of a sonorous phrase, it only confuses people. The more we cherish the memory of the Paris Commune of 1871, for instance, the less permissible is it to dismiss it with a mere reference without analysing its mistakes and the special conditions attending it. To do so would be to follow the absurd example set by the Blanquists, who were ridiculed by Engels, those Blanquists who in their "manifesto" in 1874, worshipped every action of the Commune.[30] What reply will a "Conference-ist" give to a worker who asks him what *this* "revolutionary commune" mentioned in the resolution means? He will only be able to tell him that this was the name given to a workers' government that once existed, which was unable and could not then distinguish between the elements of a democratic revolution and those of a socialist revolution, which confused the tasks of the struggle for a republic with those of the struggle for socialism, which could not carry out the task of launching an energetic military offensive against Versailles, * which made a mistake in not seizing the Bank of France, etc. In short, whether in your answer you refer to the Paris Commune or to some other commune, your answer will be: that was a government *such as ours should not be.* A fine answer, isn't it? [31] Is not the evasion of the practical programme and inappropriately beginning to give a lesson in history in a resolution evidence of the moralising of a bookworm and the helplessness of a revolutionary? Does this not reveal the very mistake which they unsuccessfully tried to accuse us of having committed, *i.e.,* of having confused democratic revolution with socialist revolution, the difference between which none of the "communes" could see?

The aim of the provisional government (so inappropriately called "commune") is declared to be "exclusively" to extend the uprising and to disrupt the government. Literally, the word "exclusively" eliminates all the other tasks; it is an echo of the absurd theory of "only from below." The elimination of the other tasks is another instance of short-sightedness and thoughtlessness. The "revolutionary commune," *i.e.,* the revolutionary government, even if only in a single city, will inevitably have to administer (even if provisionally, "partially, episodically") *all* the affairs of state, and it is the height of imprudence to hide one's head under one's wing, in this respect. This government will have to enact an eight-hour day, to establish workers' factory inspection, to provide free and universal education, to introduce the election of judges, to set up peasant committees, etc.; in a word, it will have to carry out a number of reforms. To define these reforms as "helping to extend the uprising" means juggling with words and deliberately causing greater confusion in a matter in which absolute clarity is necessary.

The concluding part of the new *Iskra* resolution does not provide any new material for criticising the trend of principles of "Economism" which has revived in our Party, but it illustrates what has been said above from a somewhat different angle.

* The headquarters of the bourgeois government and the counter-revolution during the Paris Commune of 1871.—*Ed.*

Here is that part:

Only in one event should Social-Democracy, on its own initiative, direct its efforts towards seizing power and retaining it as long as possible, namely, in the event of the revolution spreading to the advanced countries of Western Europe where conditions for the achievement of socialism have already reached a certain [?] state of maturity. In that event, the restricted historical scope of the Russian revolution can be considerably extended and the possibility of striking the path of socialist reforms will arise.

By framing its tactics in the expectation that, during the whole period of the revolution, the Social-Democratic Party will retain the position of extreme revolutionary opposition towards all the governments that succeed each other in the course of the revolution, Social-Democracy will best be able to prepare itself for using political power if it falls [??] into its hands.

The basic idea expressed here is the same as that repeatedly formulated by *Vperyod*, when it stated that we must not be afraid (as is Martynov) of a complete victory for Social-Democracy in a democratic revolution, *i.e.*, the revolutionary-democratic dictatorship of the proletariat and the peasantry, for such a victory will enable us to rouse Europe, and the socialist proletariat of Europe will then throw off the yoke of the bourgeoisie and in its turn help us to carry out a socialist revolution. But see how this idea is spoiled in the new *Iskra*-ist rendering of it. We shall not dwell on particulars—on the absurd assumption that power could "fall" into the hands of an intelligent party which considers the tactics of seizing power harmful; on the fact that the conditions for socialism in Europe have reached not a certain degree of maturity, but are already mature; on the fact that our Party programme knows of no socialist reforms but only of a socialist revolution. Let us take the principal and basic difference between the idea as presented by *Vperyod* and as presented in the resolution. *Vperyod* set a task before the revolutionary proletariat of Russia, *viz.*, to win in the battle for democracy and to use this victory for carrying revolution into Europe. The resolution fails to grasp this connection between our "decisive victory" (not in the new *Iskra* sense) and the revolution in Europe, and therefore refers, not to the tasks of the proletariat, not to the prospects of *its* victory, but to one of the possibilities in general: "in the event of the revolution spreading. . . ." *Vperyod* directly and definitely indicated, and this was incorporated in the resolution of the Third Congress of the Russian Social-Democratic Labour Party, how precisely "political power" can and must "be utilised" in the interests of the proletariat, bearing in mind what can be achieved immediately, at the given stage of social development,

69

and what must first be achieved as a democratic prerequisite for the struggle for socialism. Here, also, the resolution is hopelessly dragging at the tail when it states: "will be able to prepare itself for using," but is unable to say *in what way and how* it will be able to prepare itself, and for *what sort* of "utilisation." We have no doubt, for instance, that the new *Iskra*-ists may be "able to prepare themselves for 'using' " the leading position in the Party; but the manner in which they have utilised this position up to now and the extent to which they are prepared for this do not hold out much hope of possibility being transformed into reality.

Vperyod quite definitely stated wherein lies the real "possibility of retaining power," namely, in the revolutionary-democratic dictatorship of the proletariat and the peasantry, in their joint mass strength which is capable of outweighing all the forces of counter-revolution in the inevitable harmony of their interests in *democratic* reforms. The resolution of the Conference, however, does not give us anything positive; it merely evades the issue. Surely the possibility of retaining power in Russia must be determined by the composition of the social forces in Russia itself, by the circumstances of the democratic revolution which is now taking place in our country. The victory of the proletariat in Europe (and it is a far cry between carrying the revolution into Europe and the victory of the proletariat) will give rise to a desperate counter-revolutionary struggle of the Russian bourgeoisie—yet the resolution of the new *Iskra*-ists does not say a word about this counter-revolutionary force, the importance of which has been appraised by the resolution of the Third Congress of the Russian Social-Democratic Labour Party. If in our struggle for the republic and democracy we could not rely upon the peasantry as well as upon the proletariat, the prospect of our "retaining power" would be hopeless. And if it is not hopeless, if the "decisive victory over tsarism" opens up such a possibility, then we must say so, we must actively call for the transformation of this possibility into reality and issue practical slogans not only for the *contingency* of the revolution being carried into Europe, but also *for the purpose* of bringing this about. The appeal the tail-ist Social-Democrats make to the "restricted historical scope of the Russian revolution" only covers up their restricted comprehension of the tasks of this democratic revolution and of the role of the proletariat as the vanguard in this revolution.

One of the objections raised to the slogan "the revolutionary-democratic dictatorship of the proletariat and the peasantry" is that dictatorship presupposes a "united will" (*Iskra*, No. 95), and that there can be no united will between the proletariat and the petty bourgeoisie. This objection is fallacious, for it is based on an abstract, "metaphysical" interpretation of the term "united will." Will may be united in one respect and not united in another. The absence of unity on questions of socialism and the struggle for socialism does not prevent unity of will on questions of democracy and the struggle for a republic. To forget this would be tantamount to forgetting the logical and historical difference between a demo- cratic revolution and a socialist revolution. To forget this would mean forgetting the *national* character of the democratic revolution: if it is "national" it means that there *must* be "unity of will" pre- cisely in so far as this revolution satisfies the national needs and requirements. Beyond the boundaries of democracy there can be no unity of will between the proletariat and the peasant bourgeoisie. Class struggle between them is inevitable; but on the basis of a democratic republic this struggle will be the most far-reaching and extensive struggle of the people for *socialism*. Like everything else in the world, the revolutionary-democratic dictatorship of the prole- tariat and the peasantry has a past and a future. Its past is autocracy, serfdom, monarchy and privileges. In the struggle against this past, in the struggle against counter-revolution, a "united will" of the proletariat and the peasantry is possible, for there is unity of interests.

Its future is the struggle against private property, the struggle of the wage-worker against his master, the struggle for socialism. In this case, unity of will is impossible. * Here our path lies not from autocracy to a republic, but from a petty-bourgeois democratic re- public to socialism.

Of course, in concrete historical circumstances, the elements of the past become interwoven with those of the future, the two paths get mixed. Wage-labour and its struggle against private property exist under autocracy as well, they originate even under serfdom. But this does not prevent us from drawing a logical and historical line of demarcation between the important stages of development. Surely we all draw the distinction between bourgeois revolution and

---

* The development of capitalism which is more extensive and rapid under conditions of freedom will inevitably put a speedy end to the unity of will; the sooner the counter-revolution and reaction are crushed, the speedier will the unity of will come to an end.

socialist revolution, we all absolutely insist on the necessity of draw-ing a strict line between them; but can it be denied that in history certain particular elements of both revolutions become interwoven? Have there not been a number of socialist movements and attempts at establishing socialism in the period of democratic revolutions in Europe? And will not the future socialist revolution in Europe still have to do a great deal that has been left undone in the field of democracy?

A Social-Democrat must never, even for an instant, forget that the proletarian class struggle for socialism against the most democratic and republican bourgeoisie and petty bourgeoisie is inevitable. This is beyond doubt. From this logically follows the absolute necessity of a separate, independent and strictly class party of Social-Democ-racy. From this logically follows the provisional character of our tactics to "strike together" with the bourgeoisie and the duty to care-fully watch "our ally, as if he were an enemy," etc. All this is also beyond doubt. But it would be ridiculous and reactionary to deduce from this that we must forget, ignore or neglect those tasks which, although transient and temporary, are vital at the present time. The struggle against autocracy is a temporary and transient task of the Socialists, but to ignore or neglect this task would be tantamount to betraying socialism and rendering a service to reaction. Cer-tainly, the revolutionary-democratic dictatorship of the proletariat and the peasantry is only a transient, provisional task of the Social-ists, but to ignore this task in the period of a democratic revolution would be simply reactionary.

Concrete political tasks must be presented in concrete circum-stances. All things are relative, all things flow and are subject to change. The programme of the German Social-Democratic Party does not contain the demand for a republic. In Germany the situa-tion is such that this question can in practice hardly be separated from the question of socialism (although even as regards Germany, Engels in his comments on the draft of the Erfurt Programme of 1891 uttered a warning against belittling the importance of a re-public and of the struggle for a republic!) [32] Russian Social-Democracy never raised the question of eliminating the demand for a republic from its programme or agitation, for in our country there can be no indissoluble connection between the question of a republic and the question of socialism. It was quite natural for a German Social-Democrat of 1898 not to put the question of the republic in the forefront, and this evoked neither surprise nor condemnation. But a German Social-Democrat who in 1848 left the question of the republic in the shade would have been a downright traitor to the revolution. There is no such thing as abstract truth. Truth is always concrete.

The time will come when the struggle against Russian autocracy will be over, when the period of democratic revolution in Russia will also be over, and then it will be ridiculous to talk about "unity of will" of the proletariat and the peasantry, about a democratic dictatorship, etc. When that time comes we shall take up the question of the socialist dictatorship of the proletariat and deal with it at greater length. But at present the party of the advanced class cannot help striving in a most energetic manner for a decisive victory of the democratic revolution over tsarism. And a decisive victory is nothing else than the revolutionary-democratic dictatorship of the proletariat and the peasantry.

Author's Note to Chapter X, First Published in 1926

We would remind the reader that in the polemics between *Iskra* and *Vperyod* the former incidentally referred to Engels' letter to Turati,[33] in which Engels warned the (future) leader of the Italian reformists not to confuse the democratic revolution with the socialist revolution. The coming revolution in Italy—wrote Engels about the political situation in Italy in 1894—will be a petty-bourgeois, a democratic revolution, not a socialist revolution. *Iskra* reproached *Vperyod* with having deviated from the principle laid down by Engels. This reproach was unjust, because on the whole *Vperyod* (No. 14) fully admitted the correctness of Marx's theory on the difference between the three main forces in the revolutions of the nineteenth century. According to this theory the following forces are fighting against the old regime of autocracy, feudalism and serf-dom: (1) the liberal big bourgeoisie, (2) the radical petty bourgeoisie, (3) the proletariat. The first is fighting only for a constitutional monarchy; the second, for a democratic republic; the third, for a socialist revolution. The socialist who confuses the petty-bourgeois struggle for a complete democratic revolution with the proletarian struggle for a socialist revolution is in danger of political bankruptcy. Marx's warning in this connection is quite justified. But it is precisely for this reason that the slogan of "revolutionary communes" is wrong, because the very mistake committed by the communes that have existed in history is that they confused the democratic revolution with the socialist revolution. On the other hand, our slogan, the revolutionary-democratic dictatorship of the proletariat and the peasantry, fully safeguards us against this mistake. While absolutely recognising the bourgeois character of the revolution, which cannot *immediately* go beyond the bounds of a merely democratic revolution, our slogan *pushes forward* this particular revolution and strives to mould it into forms most advantageous to the proletariat; consequently, it strives for the utmost utilisation of the democratic revolution for a most successful further struggle of the proletariat for socialism.

XI

A Cursory Comparison Between Certain Resolutions Passed by the Third Congress of the Russian Social-Democratic Labour Party and Those Passed by the "Conference"

THE question of the provisional revolutionary government is at the present time the central point of the tactical questions of social-democracy. It is not possible, nor is there any need to dwell at equal length on the other resolutions of the Conference. We shall confine ourselves to indicating briefly a few points which confirm the above-stated basic difference between the tactical tendencies of the resolutions of the Third Congress of the Russian Social-Democratic Labour Party and those of the Conference.

Take the question of the attitude towards the tactics of the government on the eve of the revolution. Again you will find an integral answer to this question in the resolution of the Third Congress of the Russian Social-Democratic Labour Party. This resolution makes allowance for all the various conditions and tasks of the particular moment: the exposure of the hypocrisy of the government's concessions, the utilisation of even a "caricature of popular representation," the revolutionary satisfaction of the urgent demands of the working class (the eight-hour day above all), and, finally, resistance to the Black Hundreds. In the resolutions of the Conference this question is spread over several sections: "resistance to the dark forces of reaction" is only mentioned in the explanatory part of the resolution on attitude towards other parties. The participation in elections to the representative assemblies is considered separately from the "compromises" between tsarism and the bourgeoisie. Instead of calling for an eight-hour day to be achieved by revolutionary means, it passed a special resolution with the high sounding title, "On the Economic Struggle," which only repeats (after some high flown and very insipid words about "the central place occupied by the labour question in the public life of Russia") the old slogan of agitation for the "legal enactment of an eight-hour day." The inadequacy and backwardness of that slogan at the present time are too obvious to require proof.

The question of open political action: The Third Congress takes into account the forthcoming *radical* change in our activity. Secret activity and the building up of a secret apparatus must not by any means be discarded: this would mean playing into the hands of the police and would be exceedingly advantageous to the government. But even now we must think about open action. It is necessary to *prepare* immediately appropriate forms for such action and, consequently, a special apparatus—less secret—for that purpose. It is necessary to make use of the legal and semi-legal societies in order to transform them, as far as possible, into strongholds of the future, open Social-Democratic Labour Party in Russia.

On this point also the Conference split the question into fragments and failed to give a complete slogan that would cover the entire issue. The ridiculous instruction given to the Organisational Commission to concern itself with "placing" its legal publicists is especially conspicuous. The decision to subordinate to its influence "those democratic papers, which make it their aim to lend assistance to the labour movement" is altogether absurd. This is the professed object of all our legal liberal papers, nearly all of which belong to the *Osvobozhdeniye* trend. Why do not the editors of *Iskra* carry out their own advice and give us an example of how to subject *Osvobozhdeniye* to social-democratic influences? Instead of the slogan of utilising the legal unions for the creation of strongholds of the Party, we are first of all given particular advice only in regard to the "trade" unions (that all Party members must join them), and secondly, advice to guide the "revolutionary organisations of the workers" otherwise referred to as "amorphous organisations" or "revolutionary workers' clubs." How these "clubs" became amorphous organisations, what are these clubs—goodness only knows. Instead of definite and clear instructions from a supreme Party body, we get outlines of ideas and publicists' rough drafts. We do not get a complete picture of the Party beginning to pass on to a different base in its entire work.

The "peasant question" was presented by the Party Congress quite differently from the way it was presented by the Conference. The Congress drew up a resolution on the "attitude to the peasants' movement," the Conference one upon "work among the peasants." In the former, the task of guiding the wide, revolutionary, democratic movement in a nation-wide struggle against tsarism is placed in the forefront. In the latter, everything is reduced to "work" among a special stratum. In the former, a central practical slogan of agitation is advanced, namely—the immediate organisation of revolutionary peasant committees for the purpose of carrying out all the democratic reforms. In the latter, it is stated that "the demand for forming committees" must be presented to the constituent assembly. Why must we wait for this constituent assembly? Will it really be a constituent assembly? Will it be firm without first or simultaneously establishing revolutionary peasant committees? All these questions were lost sight of by the Conference. All its decisions bear the imprint of that general idea which we have traced, namely, that in the bourgeois revolution we must only carry on our special work without setting ourselves the task of guiding the whole of the democratic movement and of pursuing of it independently. Just as the Economists were constantly harping on the idea that Social-Democrats should attend to the economic struggle and the Liberals to the political struggle, so the new *Iskra*-ists throughout the whole course of their discussions, harped on the idea that we must occupy a very modest corner out of the way of the bourgeois revolution, while it is the business of the bourgeoisie to actively carry it out.

Finally, we cannot fail to note the resolution on the attitude to other parties. The resolution of the Third Congress of the Russian Social-Democratic Labour Party speaks of exposing all the limitations and inadequacies of the liberation movement carried on by the bourgeoisie, without the naive purpose of enumerating all possible instances of these limitations that may take place between Congresses, or of drawing the line between the bad and good bourgeois. The Conference, however, repeating the mistake of Starover, persistently sought to discover such a line, and expounded the famous "litmus paper" theory. Starover was moved by a good intention: to put stiffer terms to the bourgeoisie. He forgot, however, that any attempt to separate beforehand those bourgeois democrats who are worthy of approval, agreements, etc., from those who are unworthy of them, leads to a "formula" which is immediately thrown overboard by the development of events and introduces confusion into proletarian class-consciousness. The centre of gravity is shifted from real unity in the struggle to declarations, promises, slogans. Starover thought that the slogan "universal, equal, direct and secret suffrage," was a fundamental slogan. Barely two years have passed, and the "litmus paper" has proved to be useless, the slogan of universal suffrage was taken over by the *Osvobozhdeniye*-ists, who not only did not approach any nearer to social-democracy as a result of it, but, on the contrary, tried by means of this very slogan to mislead the workers and divert them from socialism.

Now the new *Iskra*-ists put forward still "stiffer conditions," they "demand" that the enemies of tsarism give "energetic and unambiguous (!?) support to all kinds of decisive actions by the organised proletariat," etc., right up to and including "active participation in the work of arming the people." The line has been drawn much farther, but it is already out of date and immediately proved to be useless. For instance, why has the slogan of a republic been omitted? Why is it that in the interests of a "ruthless revolutionary war against all the foundations of the feudal-monarchist regime," the Social-Democrats "demand" all sorts of things from the bourgeois democrats, but do not demand a republic?

That this question is not mere captiousness, that the mistake of the new *Iskra*-ists is of vital political importance . . . is proved by the "Russian Union of Liberation" (see *Proletary*, No. 4 *).

These "enemies of tsarism" would fully satisfy all the "requirements" of the new *Iskra*-ists. And yet we have shown that the spirit of *Osvobozhdeniye* is supreme in the programme (or the absence of programme) of this "Russian Union of Liberation" and that the *Osvobozhdeniye*-ists could easily take it in tow. The Conference, however, declares at the end of the resolution that "social-democracy will act as of old both against the *hypocritical friends of the people*

* *Proletary* No. 4, issued on June 17, 1905, contained a long article entitled,. "A New Revolutionary Labour Union." The article quotes the contents of the appeal issued by that union, which has adopted the name of "Russian Union of Liberation" and which set as its task to convoke a constituent assembly by means of an armed uprising. Further on the article defines the attitude of the Social-Democrats to such non-party unions. How far that union had any real importance and what its fate was during the revolution is absolutely unknown to us. . . . (Author's note to the 1908 edition.—*Ed.*)

and against all those political parties, which, though they unfurl a liberal or democratic banner, refuse to lend actual support to the revolutionary struggle of the proletariat." The "Russian Union of Liberation" not only does not refuse but insistently offers that support. Is this a guarantee that its leaders are not "hypocritical friends of the people" though they be *Osvobozhdeniye*-ists?

You see, by inventing beforehand "conditions" and presenting "demands" which are comical in their pretentious impotence, the new *Iskra*-ists at once place themselves in a ridiculous position. Their conditions and demands at once prove to be inadequate for the purpose of calculating living realities. Their quest for formulæ is hopeless, because no formulæ will detect all the various manifestations of the hypocrisy, inconsistency, and limitations of bourgeois democracy. This is not a question of a "litmus paper," nor of forms or of demands set down in writing or print, nor is it a question of distinguishing beforehand between the hypocritical and sincere "friends of the people"; it is a question of the real unity of the struggle, of social-democracy relentlessly criticising every "uncertain" step taken by bourgeois democracy. In order to bring about "the real consolidation of all the social forces interested in the democratic reconstruction" what is necessary are not the "points" over which the conference laboured so assiduously and so vainly, but the ability to advance genuinely revolutionary slogans. For this purpose we must have slogans that can raise the revolutionary and republican bourgeoisie to the level of the proletariat and not such as will reduce the tasks of the proletariat to the level of the monarchist bourgeoisie. For this purpose a most energetic participation in the uprising is necessary and not logic-chopping evasions of the urgent task of the armed uprising.

XII

WILL THE SWEEP OF THE DEMOCRATIC REVOLUTION BE DIMINISHED IF THE BOURGEOISIE DESERTS?

THE foregoing lines were already written when we received a copy of the resolution passed by the Caucasian Conference of the new *Iskra*-ists and published by *Iskra*. Better material than this *pour la bonne bouche*,* we could not wish for.

* For a titbit.—*Ed.*

The editorial board of *Iskra* quite justly remarks:

On the fundamental question of tactics, the Causacian Conference arrived at a decision *analogous* [in truth!] to the one arrived at by the All-Russian Conference [*i.e.* of the new *Iskra*-ists]. . . . On the question of the attitude of Social-Democracy towards the provisional revolutionary government, the Caucasian comrades took a very hostile position towards the new method as advocated by the *Vperyod* group and the delegates of the so-called Congress who joined it. . . . It must be admitted that the tactics of the proletarian party in a bourgeois revolution have been *very aptly* formulated by the Conference.

What is true is true. A more "apt" formulation of the fundamental error of the new *Iskra*-ists could not be invented. We shall reproduce this formula in full, first of all indicating in parentheses the blossoms, and then, later, we shall expose the fruit, as presented at the end of the formula.

RESOLUTION OF THE CAUCASIAN CONFERENCE OF NEW "ISKRA"-ISTS
ON THE PROVISIONAL REVOLUTIONARY GOVERNMENT

Considering it to be our task to take advantage of the revolutionary situation to deepen [of course! They should have added: "according to Martynov"] the Social-Democratic consciousness of the proletariat [only to deepen the consciousness, but not to establish a republic! What a "profound" conception of revolution!] in order to secure for the Party complete freedom to criticise the nascent bourgeois state system [it is not our business to secure a republic! Our business is only to secure freedom to criticise. Anarchist ideas give rise to anarchist language: "bourgeois state system"!], the Conference expresses its opposition to the formation of a Social-Democratic provisional government and to joining it [recall the resolution passed by the Bakuninists ten months before the Spanish revolution and referred to by Engels: see *Proletary*, No. 3 [34]], but considers it more expedient to exercise pressure from without [from below and not from above] upon the bourgeois provisional government in order to secure the greatest possible [?] democratisation of the state system. The Conference believes that the formation of a Social-Democratic provisional government, or entry into the government, would lead, on the one hand, to the masses of the proletariat becoming disappointed in the Social-Democratic Party and abandoning it because the Social-Democrats, in spite of the fact that they had seized power, would not be able to satisfy the pressing needs of the working class, including the establishment of socialism [the republic is not a pressing need! The authors, in their innocence, failed to observe that they were speaking in the language of anarchists, that they were speaking as if they were repudiating participation in bourgeois revolutions!], and, on the other hand, *would induce the bourgeois classes to desert the cause of the revolution and in that way diminish its sweep.*

This is where the trouble lies. This is where anarchist ideas become interwoven (as constantly occurs among West European Bernsteinians) with the purest opportunism. Just imagine: not to enter the provisional government because this will induce the bourgeoisie to desert the cause of the revolution and will thus diminish the sweep of the revolution! But here we have before us the new *Iskra* philosophy in its complete, pure and consistent form: the revolution is a bourgeois revolution, therefore we must bow to bourgeois vulgarity and make way for it. If we were guided, only partly, only for a moment, by the consideration that our participation might induce the bourgeoisie to desert the revolution, we would simply be surrendering the leadership of the revolution entirely to the bourgeois classes. By that we would place the proletariat entirely under the tutelage of the bourgeoisie (while retaining for ourselves complete "freedom to criticise"!!) and compel the proletariat to be meek and mild in order not to frighten the bourgeoisie away. We emasculate the immediate needs of the proletariat, namely, its political needs—which the Economists and their epigones have never thoroughly understood—out of fear lest the bourgeoisie be frightened away. We would completely abandon the field of the revolutionary struggle for the achievement of democracy to the extent required by the proletariat in favour of the field of bargaining with the bourgeoisie and obtaining their voluntary consent ("not to desert") at the price of our principles and of the revolution itself.

In two brief lines, the Caucasian new *Iskra*-ists managed to express the quintessence of the tactics of betraying the revolution and of converting the proletariat into a miserable hanger-on of the bourgeois classes. The mistakes of the new *Iskra*-ists which we referred to above as a tendency now stand before us elevated to the level of a clear and definite principle, *viz.*, to drag at the tail of the monarchist bourgeoisie. Because the achievement of the republic would induce (and is already inducing: Mr. Struve, for example) the bourgeoisie to desert the revolution, therefore, down with the fight for the republic! Because the bourgeoisie always and everywhere in the world is frightened by every energetic and consistent democratic demand put forward by the proletariat, therefore, hide in your dens, comrade workers; act only from without; do not dream of using the instruments and weapons of the "bourgeois state system" in the revolution and preserve for yourselves "freedom to criticise"!

The fundamental error in their conception of the term "bourgeois revolution" has come to the surface. The Martynov, new *Iskra* "conception" of the term leads directly to the betrayal of the cause of the proletariat to the bourgeoisie.

Those who have forgotten the old Economism, those who fail to study it and do not call it to mind, will find it difficult to understand the present off-shoot of Economism. Recall the Bernsteinian *Credo*.[35] From the "purely proletarian" point of view and programmes, these people deduced the following: we, Social-Democrats, are to engage in economics, in the real cause of labour, in freedom to criticise all political trickery, in genuinely deepening Social-Democratic work, whereas they, the liberals, are to engage in politics. God save us from dropping into "revolutionism"; that will frighten the bourgeoisie away. Those who read the *Credo* over again (to the very end), or the Supplement to No. 9 of *Rabochaya Mysl* * (September 1899), will be able to follow the whole of this line of reasoning.

The same thing is taking place at the present time, only on a larger scale and in application to the estimation of the whole of the "great" Russian revolution—which, alas, even beforehand, has been vulgarised and reduced to a caricature by the theoreticians of orthodox philistinism! We, Social-Democrats, are to have freedom to criticise, are to engage in deepening consciousness, to engage in actions from without. They, the bourgeois classes, must have freedom to act, a free field for revolutionary (read: liberal) leadership, the freedom to pass "reforms" from above.

These vulgarisers of Marxism have never pondered over what Marx said about the need for substituting criticism with weapons for the weapon of criticism. While they use the name of Marx in vain, they actually draw up resolutions on tactics absolutely in the spirit of the Frankfort bourgeois chatterboxes, who freely criticised absolutism, deepened democratic consciousness, but failed to understand the fact that the time of revolution is a time of action, both from above and from below. In converting Marxism into a subject for hair-splitting, they have converted the ideology of the most advanced, most determined and energetic revolutionary class into the ideology of its most undeveloped strata, which shrink from difficult revolutionary-democratic tasks and leave them to be solved by the Struves.

If the bourgeois classes desert the revolution because the Social-Democrats join the revolutionary government, they will thereby "diminish" the sweep of the revolution.

---

* *Workers' Thought*, the most consistent organ of Economism, appearing between October 1897 and December 1902 in Berlin and Petersburg.—*Ed.*

Do you hear this, Russian workers! The sweep of the revolution will be mightier if it is carried out by the Struves, who must not be frightened away by the Social-Democrats and who want, not victory over tsarism, but to strike a bargain with it. The sweep of the revolution will be stronger if, of the two possible outcomes which we have outlined above, the first comes about, *i.e.*, if the monarchist bourgeoisie come to an understanding with the autocracy concerning a "constitution" *à la* Shipov.

Social-Democrats who write such shameful things in resolutions intended for the guidance of the whole Party, or who approve of such "apt" resolutions, are so absorbed in their hair-splitting, which crushes the living spirit of Marxism, that they fail to observe how these resolutions convert all their other excellent words into mere phrasemongering. Take any of their articles in *Iskra*, or take the notorious pamphlet written by our celebrated Martynov, and there you will read about *people's* rebellion, about carrying the revolution to the *very* end, about striving to rely upon the lower strata of the people in the fight against the inconsistent bourgeoisie. But all these excellent things become miserable phrasemongering immediately you accept or approve of the idea about "the sweep of the revolution" being "'diminished" if the bourgeoisie abandon it. One of two things, gentlemen: either we, together with the people, strive to bring about the revolution and obtain complete victory over tsarism, *in spite of* the inconsistent, selfish and cowardly bourgeoisie, or we do not accept this "in spite of," we do fear that the bourgeoisie will "desert" the revolution. In the latter case we betray the proletariat and the people to the bourgeoisie, to the inconsistent, selfish and cowardly bourgeoisie.

Don't make any attempt to misinterpret what I have said. Don't start howling that you are being charged with deliberate treachery. No, you have been crawling all the time and have now crawled into the mire as unconsciously as the Economists crawled into it, drawn inexorably and irrevocably down the inclined plane of making Marxism more "profound," to anti-revolutionary, soulless and lifeless efforts at "wisdom."

Have you ever considered, gentlemen, what the real social forces that determine the "sweep of the revolution" are? Let us leave aside the forces of foreign politics, of international combinations, which have turned out favourably for us at the present time, but which we leave out of our discussion, and quite rightly so, in so far as we are discussing the internal forces of Russia. Look at the internal social forces. Against the revolution are rallied the autocracy, the Court, the police, the government officials, the army and a handful of the higher aristocracy. The deeper the indignation of the people becomes, the less reliable become the troops, and the more the government officials begin to waver. Moreover, the bourgeoisie, on the whole, is now in favour of the revolution, makes zealous speeches about liberty, and more and more frequently talks in the name of the people, and even in the name of the revolution.* But we Marxists all know from our theories and from daily and hourly observations of our liberals, Zemstvo councillors and followers of *Osvobozhdeniye* that the bourgeoisie is inconsistent, selfish and cowardly in its support of the revolution. The bourgeoisie, in the mass, will inevitably turn towards counter-revolution, towards autocracy, against the revolution and against the people, immediately its narrow selfish interests are met, immediately it "deserts" consistent democracy (*it is already deserting it!*). There remains the "people," that is, the proletariat and the peasantry. The proletariat alone is capable of marching reliably to the end, for its goal lies far beyond the democratic revolution. That is why the proletariat fights in the front ranks for the republic and contemptuously rejects silly and unworthy advice to take care not to frighten the bourgeoisie. The peasantry consists of a great number of semi-proletarian as well as petty-bourgeois elements. This causes it also to waver and compels the proletariat to close its ranks in a strictly class party. But the instability of the peasantry differs radically from the instability of the bourgeoisie, for at the present time the peasantry is interested not so much in the absolute preservation of private property as in the confiscation of the landlords' land, one of the principal forms of private property. While this does not cause the peasantry to become socialist or cease to be petty-bourgeois it may cause them to become whole-hearted and most radical adherents of the democratic revolution. The peasantry will inevitably become such if only the progress of revolutionary events, which is enlightening it, is not interrupted too soon by the treachery of the bourgeoisie and the defeat of the proletariat. Subject to this condition, the peasantry will inevitably become a bulwark of the revo-

* In this connection the open letter by Mr. Struve to Jaurès, recently published by the latter in *L'Humanité* and by the former in *Osvobozhdeniye*, No. 72, is very interesting.

lution and the republic, for only a completely victorious revolution can give the peasantry *everything* in the sphere of agrarian reforms —*everything* that the peasants desire, of which they dream, and of which they truly stand in need (not for the abolition of capitalism as the "Socialist-Revolutionaries" imagine, but) in order to raise themselves out of the mire of semi-serfdom, out of the gloom of oppression and servitude, in order to improve their conditions of life as far as it is possible to improve them under commodity production.

Moreover, the peasantry is drawn to the revolution not only by the prospect of a radical agrarian reform but by its general and permanent interests. Even in its fight against the proletariat, the peasantry stands in need of democracy, for only a democratic system is capable of exactly expressing its interests and of ensuring its predominance as the mass and the majority. The more enlightened the peasantry becomes (and since the Japanese War it is becoming enlightened at a much more rapid pace than those who are accustomed to measuring enlightenment by the school standard suspect), the more consistent and determined will it be in its support of the complete democratic revolution; for, unlike the bourgeoisie, it has nothing to fear from the supremacy of the people, but, on the contrary, can only gain by it. The democratic republic will become the ideal of the peasantry as soon as it frees itself from its naive monarchism, because the conscious monarchism of the bourgeois brokers (with an upper chamber, etc.) implies for the peasantry the same disfranchisement and the same ignorance and oppression as it suffers from today, only slightly polished with the varnish of European constitutionalism.

That is why the bourgeoisie as a class naturally and inevitably strives to come under the wing of the liberal-monarchist party, while the peasantry, in the mass, strives to come under the leadership of the revolutionary and republican party. That is why the bourgeoisie is incapable of carrying the democratic revolution to its ultimate conclusion, while the peasantry is capable of carrying the revolution to the end; and we must exert all our efforts to help to do so.

It may be objected: but there is no need to argue about this, this is all A B C; all Social-Democrats understand this perfectly well. But that is not so. Those who can talk about "the sweep" of the revolution being "diminished" because the bourgeoisie will desert it do not understand this. These people simply repeat by rote the words of our agrarian programme without understanding their meaning, for otherwise they would not be frightened by the concept of the revolutionary-democratic dictatorship of the proletariat and the peasantry, which follows logically from the Marxian philosophy and from our programme; otherwise they would not restrict the sweep of the great Russian revolution to the limits to which the bourgeoisie are prepared to go. These people defeat their abstract Marxian revolutionary phrases by their concrete anti-Marxian and anti-revolutionary resolutions.

Those who really understand the role of the peasantry in the victorious Russian revolution would not dream of saying that the sweep of the revolution would be diminished if the bourgeoisie deserted it. For, as a matter of fact, the Russian revolution will assume its real sweep, and will really assume the widest revolutionary sweep possible in the epoch of bourgeois-democratic revolution, only when the bourgeoisie deserts it and when the masses of the peasantry come out as active revolutionaries side by side with the proletariat. In order that it may be carried to its logical conclusion, our democratic revolution must rely on such forces as are capable of paralysing the inevitable inconsistency of the bourgeoisie (*i.e.*, actually to "induce it to desert the revolution," which the Caucasian adherents of *Iskra* fear so much because they fail to think things out).

The proletariat must carry out to the end the democratic revolution, and in this unite to itself the mass of the peasantry in order to crush by force the resistance of the autocracy and to paralyse the instability of the bourgeoisie. The proletariat must accomplish the socialist revolution and in this unite with itself the mass of the semi-proletarian elements of the population in order to crush by force the resistance of the bourgeoisie and to paralyse the instability of the peasantry and petty bourgeoisie. Such are the tasks of the proletariat which the new *Iskra*-ists, in their arguments and resolutions about the sweep of the revolution, present in such a narrow manner.

One circumstance, however, must not be forgotten, although it is frequently lost sight of when arguing about the "sweep" of the revolution. It must not be forgotten that what is at issue is not the difficulties of the task, but where to seek for and achieve its solution. The question is not whether it is difficult or not to make the sweep of the revolution powerful and invincible, but how we are to act in order to enlarge the sweep of the revolution. The difference of opinion affects precisely the fundamental character of our activity, its very direction. We emphasize this because careless and dishonest people too frequently confuse two different questions, namely, the question of the direction in which the road is leading, *i.e.*, the selection of one of two roads, and the question of the ease with which the goal can be reached, or how near the goal is on the given road.

We have not dealt with this last question at all because it has not raised any disagreement or divergency in the Party. But it goes without saying that the question is extremely important in itself and deserves the most serious attention of all Social-Democrats. It would be a piece of unpardonable optimism to forget the difficulties which accompany the task of drawing into the movement not only the mass of the working class, but of the peasantry as well. These difficulties have more than once been the rock against which all the efforts to carry a democratic revolution to its end have been wrecked. And always it was the inconsistent and selfish bourgeoisie which triumphed, because it both "made money" in the shape of monarchist protection against the people, and "preserved the virginity" of liberalism, or of *Osvobozhdeniye*-ism. But the fact that difficulties exist does not mean that these difficulties are insurmountable. What is important is to be convinced that the path chosen is the correct one, and this conviction will multiply a hundredfold the revolutionary energy and revolutionary enthusiasm which can perform miracles.

How deep is the gulf that divides Social-Democrats today on the question of the path to be chosen can immediately be seen by comparing the Caucasian resolution of the new *Iskra*-ists with the resolution of the Third Congress of the Russian Social-Democratic Labour Party. The resolution of the Congress says that the bourgeoisie is inconsistent; it will invariably try to deprive us of the gains of the revolution. Therefore, make energetic preparations for the fight, comrades and fellow-workers! Arm yourselves, bring the peasantry to your side! We shall not surrender the gains of the revolution to the selfish bourgeoisie without a fight. The resolution of the Caucasian new *Iskra*-ists says: the bourgeoisie is inconsistent, it may desert the revolution. Therefore, comrades and fellow-workers, please do not think of joining the provisional government, for if you do, the bourgeoisie will surely desert the revolution, and the sweep of the revolution will therefore become diminished.

One side says: push the revolution forward to its very end, in spite of the resistance of the passivity of the inconsistent bourgeoisie.

The other side says: do not think of carrying the revolution to the end independently, for if you do, the inconsistent bourgeoisie will desert it.

Are these not two diametrically opposite paths? Is it not obvious that one set of tactics absolutely excludes the other? Is it not clear that the first tactics are the only correct tactics of revolutionary Social-Democracy, while the second are in fact purely *Osvobozhdeniye* tactics?

XIII

Conclusion. Dare We Win?

Those who are superficially acquainted with the state of affairs in the ranks of Russian Social-Democracy, or those who judge by appearances without knowing the history of our internal Party struggle since the days of Economism, very often dismiss even the tactical disagreements which have now become crystallised, especially after the Third Congress, by arguing that there are two natural, inevitable and quite reconcilable trends in every Social-Democratic movement. They say that one side lays special emphasis on the ordinary, current, everyday work, on the necessity of developing propaganda and agitation, of preparing forces, deepening the movement, etc., while the other side lays emphasis on the fighting, general, political, revolutionary tasks of the movement, on the necessity of an armed uprising and of advancing the slogans: revolutionary-democratic dictatorship and provisional revolutionary government. Neither side should exaggerate, they say, extremes are bad, both here and there (and, generally speaking, everywhere in the world), etc., etc.

But the cheap truths of worldly (and "political" in quotation marks) wisdom, which are undoubtedly contained in such arguments, too often cover up a lack of comprehension of the urgent, acute needs of the Party. Take the present tactical differences among Russian Social-Democrats. Of course, the special emphasis laid on the everyday side of work, such as we observe in the new *Iskra*-ist arguments about tactics, does not in itself present any danger and would not give rise to any difference of opinion regarding tactical slogans. But the moment you compare the resolutions of the Third Congress of the Russian Social-Democratic Labour Party with the resolutions of the Conference this difference becomes strikingly obvious.

And what is the reason? The reason is that, in the first place, it is not enough to point in an abstract way to the two trends in the movement and to the harmlessness of extremes. It is necessary to know concretely what the given movement is suffering from at the given time, where the real political danger for the Party lies at the present time. Secondly, it is necessary to know what real political forces are receiving grist for their mill from these tactical slogans or perhaps the absence of slogans. If you listen to the new *Iskra*-ists you will arrive at the conclusion that the Social-Democratic Party is faced with the danger of throwing overboard propaganda and agitation, the economic struggle and the criticism of bourgeois democracy, of being inordinately attracted to military preparations, armed attacks, the seizure of power, etc. But in fact real danger is threatening the Party from a very different quarter. Those who are more or less familiar with the state of the movement, those who follow it carefully and intelligently, cannot fail to see the ridiculous side of the new *Iskra's* fears. The whole work of the Russian Social-Democratic Labour Party has already been moulded into solid immutable forms which absolutely guarantee that our main attention will be fixed on propaganda and agitation, impromptu and mass meetings, the distribution of leaflets and pamphlets, assistance to the economic struggle and the adoption of the slogans of that struggle. There is not a single committee of the Party, not a single district committee, not a single central meeting or a single factory group where ninety-nine per cent of all the attention, energy and time are not constantly devoted to the performance of these functions, which have taken root ever since the middle of the 'nineties of the last century. Only those who are altogether ignorant of the movement do not know this. Only very naive or ill-informed people can take the new *Iskra*-ists seriously when they, with an air of great importance, repeat stale truths.

The fact is that not only is no excessive zeal displayed among us in regard to the tasks of the uprising, the general political slogans and the task of leading the national revolution, but, on the contrary, it is precisely the *backwardness* in this respect that is most striking, for that is our weakest spot and a real danger to the movement which may degenerate and in some places does degenerate into a movement that is no longer revolutionary in deeds, but only in words. Of the many hundreds of organisations, groups and circles carrying on the work of the Party you will not find a single one which, from its very formation, has not carried on everyday work— the kind of everyday work which the wiseacres of the new *Iskra* now talk about as if they have discovered new truths. On the other hand, you will find an insignificant percentage of groups and circles which have understood the tasks of an armed uprising, which have started to carry them out, which have become convinced of the necessity of leading the national revolution against tsarism, of the necessity of advancing for that purpose precisely such and no other progressive slogans.

We are lagging behind terribly in the fulfilment of the progressive and the genuinely revolutionary tasks; in very many instances we have not even become conscious of them, here and there we have allowed revolutionary bourgeois democracy to become strong because of our backwardness in this respect. And the writers in the new *Iskra* turn their backs on the course of events and on the requirements of the time, and persistently repeat: Don't forget the old! Don't let yourselves be carried away by the new! This is the main, the invariable *leitmotif* of all the important resolutions of the Conference; whereas the Congress resolutions repeat with equal persistency: confirming the old (and without stopping to chew it over and over precisely because it is old and has been settled and recorded in literature, in resolutions and by experience) we put forward a new task, draw attention to it, proclaim a new slogan, and demand that the genuinely revolutionary Social-Democrats immediately set to work to fulfil it.

That is how matters really stand with regard to the question of the two trends in Social-Democratic tactics. The revolutionary epoch has put forward new tasks which only the totally blind can fail to see. Some Social-Democrats definitely recognise these tasks and put them on the order of the day: an armed uprising is a most pressing need, prepare yourselves for it immediately and energetically, remember that this is necessary in order to attain decisive victory, advance the slogans of the republic, of the provisional government, of the revolutionary-democratic dictatorship of the proletariat and the peasantry. Others, on the other hand, draw back, mark time, write prefaces instead of advancing slogans; instead of pointing out the new while confirming the old, they tediously chew the old over and over again at great length, invent subterfuges to avoid the new, and are unable to determine the conditions of decisive victory or of advancing such slogans as alone would correspond to the striving for a final victory.

The political result of this tailism is now apparent. The fairy tale about rapprochement between the "majority" of the Russian Social-Democratic Labour Party and revolutionary-bourgeois democracy remains a fable which has not been confirmed by a single political fact, by a single important resolution of the "Bolsheviks" or a single act of the Third Congress of the Russian Social-Democratic Labour Party. Meanwhile, the opportunist, monarchist bourgeoisie, as represented by *Osvobozhdeniye* has for a long time past been *welcoming* the trend of "principles" of the new *Iskra*-ists and now it is actually running its mill with the grist which the latter bring, is adopting their catch-words and "ideas" in opposition to "conspiracy" and "riots," against exaggerating the "technical" side of the revolution, against directly proclaiming the slogan of an armed uprising, against the "revolutionism" of the extreme demands, etc., etc. The resolution of a whole conference of "Menshevik" Social-Democrats in the Caucasus and the endorsement of that resolution by the editors of the new *Iskra* sums it all up politically in an unmistakable way: we fear the bourgeoisie will desert if the proletariat takes part in the revolutionary-democratic dictatorship! This explains everything. This definitely transforms the proletariat into an appendage of the monarchist bourgeoisie. This proves in deeds, not by a casual declaration of some individual, but by a resolution especially endorsed by a whole trend, the *political significance* of the tailism of the new *Iskra*.

Whoever ponders over these facts will understand the real significance of the now fashionable reference to the two sides and the two trends in the Social-Democratic movement. Take Bernsteinism, for example, for the study of these trends on a large scale. The Bernsteinists in exactly the same way have been dinning into our ears that it is they who understand the true needs of the proletariat, the task of its growing forces, of intensifying the whole work, of training the elements of a new society, of propaganda and agitation. Bernstein says: we demand a frank recognition of the situation! And by that he sanctions a "movement" *without* "final aims," sanctions defensive tactics only, preaches the tactics of fear "lest the bourgeoisie desert." The Bernsteinists also raised an outcry against the "Jacobinism" of the revolutionary Social-Democrats, against the "publicists" who fail to understand the "initiative of the workers," etc., etc. In reality, as everyone knows, the revolutionary Social-Democrats never thought of abandoning the everyday, petty work, the training of forces, etc., etc. All they demanded was a clear understanding of the final aim, a clear presentation of revolutionary tasks; they wanted to raise the semi-proletarian and semi-petty-bourgeois strata to the revolutionary level of the proletariat, not to degrade the latter to the opportunist consideration of "lest the bourgeoisie desert." Perhaps the most striking expression of his difference between the intellectual opportunist wing and the proletarian revolutionary wing of the Party was the question: *dürfen wir siegen?* "dare we win?" Is it permissible for us to win? Would not such victory be dangerous to us? Ought we to win? [36] This at first sight strange question was raised, however, and had to be raised, because the opportunists were afraid of victory, were frightening the proletariat away from it, were prophesying various evils that would result from it, were scoffing at the slogans which directly called for victory.

The same fundamental division between the intellectual-opportunist trend and the proletarian-revolutionary trend exists also among us, with the very important difference, however, that here we are faced with the question of a democratic revolution, and not of a socialist revolution. The question "dare we win?", absurd as it may seem at first sight, has also been raised here. It was raised by Martynov in his *Two Dictatorships* in which he prophesied dire misfortune if we make effective preparations for and successfully carry out an uprising. The question has been presented in the whole of the new *Iskra* literature dealing with the provisional revolutionary government, and in this connection persistent, though futile, efforts have been made continually to confuse the participation of Millerand in a bourgeois-opportunist government with the participation of Varlin * in a petty-bourgeois revolutionary government. It was clinched by the resolution "lest the bourgeoisie desert." And although Kautsky, for instance, now tries to wax ironical about

---

* Louis Eugène Varlin (1840-1871), a worker and member of the Paris Commune.—*Ed.*

our disputes concerning a provisional revolutionary government, and says that it is like dividing the bear's skin before the bear is killed,[37] this irony only proves that even intelligent and revolutionary Social-Democrats miss the point when they talk about something they know only by hearsay. German Social-Democracy is a long way from killing its bear (carrying out a socialist revolution) but the dispute as to whether we "dare" kill our bear was of enormous importance from the point of view of principles and of practical politics. Russian Social-Democrats are not yet by any means strong enough to "kill their bear" (to carry out a democratic revolution) but the question as to whether we "dare" kill it is of extreme importance for the whole future of Russia and for the future of Russian Social-Democracy. An army cannot be energetically and successfully recruited and guided unless we are sure that we "dare" win.

Take our old "Economists." They too raised an outcry that their opponents were conspirators, Jacobins (see *Rabocheye Dyelo*, especially No. 10, and Martynov's speech in the debates on the programme at the Second Congress) who by plunging into politics were divorcing themselves from the masses, forgetting the fundamentals of the labour movement, ignoring the initiative of the workers, etc., etc. In reality these supporters of "the initiative of the workers" were opportunist intellectuals who tried to foist on the workers their own narrow and philistine conception of the tasks of the proletariat. In reality the opponents of Economism, as everyone can see from the old *Iskra*, did not neglect or put into the background any of the items of Social-Democratic work, did not forget the economic struggle; but they were able simultaneously to present the urgent and immediate political tasks in their full scope, and to oppose the transformation of the party of the workers into an "economic" appendage of the liberal bourgeoisie.

The Economists have learned by rote that politics are based on economics and "understood" this to mean that the political struggle should be reduced to the economic struggle. The new *Iskra*-ists have learned by rote that the economic basis of the democratic revolution is the bourgeois revolution, and "understood" this to mean that the democratic tasks of the proletariat must be degraded to the level of bourgeois moderation and must not exceed the boundaries beyond which the "bourgeoisie will desert." On the pretext of deepening their work, on the pretext of rousing "the initiative of the workers" and defending a pure class policy the Economists, in fact, delivered the working class into the hands of the liberal-bourgeois politicians, *i.e.*, were leading the Party along a path which objectively meant that. The new *Iskra*-ists on the same pretext are in fact betraying the interests of the proletariat in the democratic revolution to the bourgeoisie, *i.e.*, are leading the Party along a path which objectively means that. The Economists thought that it was not the business of Social-Democrats to lead the struggle, but the business of the liberals. The new *Iskra*-ists think that it is not the business of the Social-Democrats actively to bring about the democratic revolution, but really that of the democratic bourgeoisie, for, they argue, if the proletariat takes a preponderant part in the revolution and leads it, this will "restrict the sweep" of the revolution.

In short, the new *Iskra*-ists are the epigones of Economism, not only by virtue of their origin at the Second Party Congress, but also by their present manner of presenting the tactical tasks of the proletariat in the democratic revolution. They, too, represent an intellectual-opportunist wing of the Party. In the sphere of organisation they began with the anarchist individualism of the intellectuals and finished with "disorganisation-process," and the "rules" adopted by the Conference permit Party literature to be separated from the Party organisation, introduce an indirect and almost four-stage system of elections, a system of Bonapartist plebiscites instead of democratic representation, and finally the principle of "agreement" between the part and the whole. In Party tactics they slipped down on the same inclined plane. In the "plan of the Zemstvo campaign" they declared that the sending of deputations to Zemstvo members was the "higher type of demonstration," since they could discover only two active forces operating on the political scene (on the eve of January 22 [9]!)—the government and bourgeois democracy. They made the urgent task of arming the people "more profound" by substituting for the direct practical slogan to arm, the slogan to arm the people with a burning desire to arm themselves. The problems of an armed uprising, of the provisional government and of the revolutionary-democratic dictatorship are now distorted and weakened in their official resolutions. "Lest the bourgeoisie desert," this final chord of their last resolution, throws a glaring light on the question as to whither their path is leading the Party.

The democratic revolution in Russia is bourgeois in its social and economic content. But it is not enough simply to repeat this correct

Marxian postulate. It must be understood and applied in political slogans. Generally speaking, all political liberties secured on the basis of the present, *i.e.*, capitalist, relations of production are bourgeois liberties. The demand for political liberties expresses first of all the interests of the bourgeoisie. Its representatives were the first to put forward this demand. Its supporters have everywhere used the liberties they acquired like masters, and have reduced them to moderate and exact bourgeois doses, combining them with the suppression of the revolutionary proletariat by methods most refined in peace time and brutally cruel in times of storm.

But only the Narodnik rebels, anarchists and also Economists could deduce from this that the struggle for liberty must be rejected or degraded. These intellectual philistine doctrines could be foisted on the proletariat only for a time and against its will. The proletariat always instinctively realised that it needed political liberty more than anyone else, in spite of the fact that its immediate effect would be to strengthen and to organise the bourgeoisie. The proletariat seeks its salvation not by avoiding the class struggle, but by developing it, by extending its scope, its own class consciousness, organisation and determination. The Social-Democrat who debases the tasks of the political struggle becomes transformed from a tribune of the people into a trade union secretary. The Social-Democrat who debases the proletarian tasks in a democratic bourgeois revolution becomes transformed from a leader of the people's revolution into a mere leader of a free labour union.

Yes, the *people's* revolution. Social-Democracy has justly fought and continues to fight against the bourgeois-democratic abuse of the word "people." It demands that this word shall not be used to cover up a failure to understand the significance of class antagonisms. It absolutely insists on the need for complete class independence for the party of the proletariat. But it divides the "people" into "classes," not in order that the advanced class may become self-centred, or confine itself to narrow aims and restrict its activity so as not to frighten the economic masters of the world, but in order that the advanced class, which does not suffer from the half-heartedness, vacillation and indecision of the intermediate classes, shall with all the greater energy and enthusiasm fight for the cause of the whole of the people, at the head of the whole of the people.

That is precisely what the contemporary new *Iskra*-ists, who instead of advancing active political slogans in a democratic revolution only repeat in a moralising way the word "class," parsed in all genders and cases, fail to understand.

The democratic revolution is a bourgeois revolution. The slogan of Black Redistribution of the land, or "land and liberty"—this most widespread slogan of the peasant masses, down-trodden, and ignorant, yet passionately yearning for light and happiness—is a bourgeois slogan. But we Marxists must know that there is not, nor can there be, any other path to real freedom for the proletariat and the peasantry than the path of bourgeois freedom and bourgeois progress. We must not forget that there is not, nor can there be at the present time, any other means of bringing socialism nearer than by complete political liberty, a democratic republic, a revolutionary-democratic dictatorship of the proletariat and the peasantry. Being the representatives of the advanced and of the only revolutionary class, revolutionary without reservations, doubts and retrospection, we must present to the whole of the people the tasks of a democratic revolution as widely and as boldly as possible, and display the maximum of initiative in so doing. The degradation of these tasks, theoretically, is tantamount to making a caricature of Marxism, tantamount to a philistine distortion of it. In practical politics it is tantamount to delivering the cause of the revolution into the hands of the bourgeoisie, which will inevitably shirk the task of consistently carrying out the revolution. The difficulties that lie on the road to the complete victory of the revolution are enormous. No one could blame the representatives of the proletariat if, having done everything in their power, their efforts are defeated by the resistance of the reaction, the treachery of the bourgeoisie and the ignorance of the masses. But everybody, and the class conscious proletariat above all, will condemn Social-Democracy if it restricts the revolutionary energy of the democratic revolution and dampens revolutionary enthusiasm by the fear of winning, fear "lest the bourgeoisie deserts."

Revolutions are the locomotives of history, said Marx. Revolutions are the festivals of the oppressed and the exploited. At no other time are the masses of the people in a position to come forward so actively as creators of a new social order as at a time of revolution. At such times the people are capable of performing miracles, if judged by a narrow philistine scale of gradual progress. But the leaders of the revolutionary parties must also, at such a time, present their tasks in a wider and bolder fashion, so that their slogan may always be in advance of the revolutionary initiative of the masses, serve them as a beacon and reveal to them our democratic and socialist ideal in all its magnitude and splendour, indicate the shortest, the most direct route to complete, absolute and final victory. Let us leave to the opportunists of the *Osvobozhdeniye* bourgeoisie the task of seeking circuitous paths of compromise out of fear of the revolution and of the direct path. If we are compelled by force to drag along such paths, we shall know how to fulfil our duty in petty, everyday work. But let the ruthless struggle first decide the path we ought to take. We shall be traitors to and betrayers of the revolution if we do not use the festive energy of the masses and their revolutionary enthusiasm in order to wage a ruthless and unflinching struggle for a straight and determined path. Let the bourgeois opportunists contemplate the future reaction with cowardly fear. The workers will not be frightened either by the thought that the reaction proposes to be terrible or by the thought that the bourgeoisie proposes to desert. The workers are not looking forward to striking bargains, they do not ask for sops; they are striving to crush the reactionary forces mercilessly, *i.e.*, to set up a *revolutionary-democratic dictatorship of the proletariat and the peasantry.*

Of course, greater dangers threaten the ship of our Party in stormy times than in periods of smooth "sailing," in periods of liberal progress, which means the painfully slow sweating of the working class by its exploiters. Of course, the tasks of a revolutionary-democratic dictatorship are a thousand times more difficult and more complicated than the tasks of an "extreme opposition" or of the exclusively parliamentary struggle. But those who in the present revolutionary situation are consciously capable of preferring smooth sailing and the path of safe "opposition" had better abandon Social-Democratic work for a while; let them wait until the revolution is over, when the feast days will have passed, when humdrum everyday life starts again, when their narrow humdrum point of view no longer strikes such an abominably discordant note, or constitutes such an ugly distortion of the tasks of the advanced class.

At the head of the whole of the people, and particularly of the peasantry—for complete freedom, for the consistent democratic revolution, for a republic! At the head of all the toilers and the exploited—for socialism! Such must in practice be the policy of the revolutionary proletariat, such is the class slogan which must permeate and determine the solution of every tactical question, and every practical step of the workers' party during the revolution.

June-July 1905.

POSTSCRIPT

ONCE MORE ABOUT THE *Osvobozhdeniye* AND THE NEW *Iskra* TRENDS

The issues Nos. 71-72 of *Osvobozhdeniye* and Nos. 102-103 of *Iskra* provide a wealth of additional material on the question to which we have devoted chapter 8 of our pamphlet. Since we are unable to use all of this rich material here, we shall dwell only on the most important points: first, the kind of "realism" in Social-Democracy *Osvobozhdeniye* praises and why it must praise it, and, secondly, the interrelation between the concepts: revolution and dictatorship.

I. WHY DO THE BOURGEOIS-LIBERAL REALISTS PRAISE THE SOCIAL-DEMOCRATIC "REALISTS"?

The articles, "The Split in Russian Social-Democracy" and "The Triumph of Common Sense" (*Osvobozhdeniye*, No. 72) present the opinions of the representatives of the liberal bourgeoisie about Social-Democracy, which are of exceptional value for class-conscious proletarians. We cannot too strongly recommend every Social-Democrat reading these articles in full and *pondering* over every sentence in them. We shall reproduce first of all the principal propositions contained in both these articles.

Osvobozhdeniye states:

An outside observer will experience considerable difficulty in grasping the real political meaning of the differences that have split the Social-Democratic Party into two factions. To define the majority faction as the more radical and straightforward and the minority as the one which allows certain compromises in the interests of the cause would not be quite correct, and in any case would not provide an exhaustive characterisation. At any rate the traditional dogmas of Marxist orthodoxy are observed by the minority faction with even greater zeal perhaps than by the Lenin faction. The following characterisation would appear to us to be more accurate. The fundamental political mood of the majority is abstract revolutionism, rebelliousness, a striving to rouse rebellion among the masses of the people by any means available and immediately to seize power in their name; this, to a certain extent, brings the Leninists closer to the Socialist-Revolutionaries, and in their minds the idea of class struggle is obscured by the idea of an all-national Russian revolution; while renouncing in practice much of the narrow-mindedness of Social-Democratic doctrine, the

Leninists on the other hand are deeply imbued with the narrow-mindedness of revolutionism; renouncing all other practical work except the preparation of an immediate uprising, they on principle ignore all forms of legal and semi-legal agitation and all kinds of practically useful compromises with other oppositional trends. The minority, on the other hand, while holding fast to the dogma of Marxism, at the same time preserves the realist elements of Marxist philosophy. The fundamental idea of this faction is the antagonism of interests between the proletariat and the bourgeoisie. But on the other hand, the proletarian struggle is conceived, of course, within certain limits set by the immutable dogmas of Social-Democracy—in a realistically sober fashion, with a clear perception of all the concrete conditions and tasks of this struggle. Neither of the factions pursue their respective fundamental points of view quite consistently, for in their ideological, political activity they are bound by the strict formulae of the Social-Democratic catechism which prevents the Leninists from becoming out and out rebels like, at any rate, some of the Socialist-Revolutionaries, and the *Iskra*-ists from becoming practical leaders of a real working class political movement.

After quoting the contents of the principal resolutions the writer in *Osvobozhdeniye* illustrates with a few concrete remarks his general "ideas" with regard to them. He states that "the attitude of the minority Conference towards armed uprising is totally different from that of the Third Congress." "The attitude towards an armed uprising" explains the differences in the respective resolutions on the provisional government.

The same difference is revealed also in regard to the trade unions. The Leninists did not say a single word in their resolution about this most important starting point in the political education and organisation of the working class. On the contrary, the minority drew up a very serious resolution.

Both factions are unanimous in regard to the Liberals, says the writer, but the Third Congress

repeats almost word for word Plekhanov's resolution on the attitude towards the Liberals passed by the Second Congress and rejects Starover's resolution, adopted by the same Congress which was more favourable to the Liberals.... . Although the Congress and the Conference are, on the whole, agreed in their resolutions on the peasant movement, the majority lays more emphasis on the idea of the revolutionary confiscation of the land of the landlords, etc., while the minority wants to make the demand for democratic state and administrative reforms the basis of its agitation.

Finally, *Osvobozhdeniye* cites from *Iskra*, No. 100, a Menshevik resolution, the main point of which reads as follows:

In view of the fact that at the present time underground work alone does not secure the adequate participation of the masses in party life and partly leads to a contrast being drawn between the masses, as such, and the Party as an illegal organisation, the latter must undertake the leadership of the economic struggles of the workers on a legal basis and strictly connect this struggle with Social-Democratic tasks.

On this resolution *Osvobozhdeniye* exclaims:

We heartily welcome this resolution as a triumph of common sense, as evidence that a certain section of the Social-Democratic Party is beginning to see the light on tactics.

The reader is now in possession of the main opinions of *Osvobozhdeniye*. It would be a great mistake, of course, to regard these opinions as being correct, in the sense that they correspond to objective truth. Every Social-Democrat will easily detect mistakes in them at every step. It would be naïve to forget that all these opinions are so deeply imbued with the interests and the views of the liberal bourgeoisie, that in this sense they are thoroughly biased and tendentious. They reflect the views of Social-Democracy in the same way as a concave or convex mirror reflects objects. But it would be a still greater mistake to forget that in the final analysis, these distorted bourgeois opinions reflect the real interests of the bourgeoisie, which, as a class, undoubtedly understands correctly which trends in Social-Democracy are of advantage to it, nearer, more akin and sympathetic to it, and which trends are harmful to it, distant, alien and antipathetic to it. No bourgeois philosopher or bourgeois publicist can ever understand Social-Democracy properly, be it the Menshevik or the Bolshevik variety. But a more or less sensible publicist will not be deceived by his class instinct, and will always grasp, on the whole correctly, the importance for the bourgeoisie of this or that trend in Social-Democracy, although he may present it in a distorted way. Therefore, the class instinct of our enemy, his class opinion, always deserves the very serious attention of every class-conscious proletarian.

What then does the class instinct of the Russian bourgeoisie, as expressed by the *Osvobozhdeniye*-ists, tell us?

It quite definitely expresses its satisfaction with the tendencies of new *Iskra*-ism, praises it for its realism, sobriety, the triumph of common sense, the seriousness of its resolutions, tactical enlightenment, practicalness, etc., and it expresses dissatisfaction with the tendencies of the Third Congress, censures it for its narrow-mindedness, revolutionism, rebelliousness, for rejecting practically useful compromises, etc. The class instinct of the bourgeoisie suggests to it precisely what has been repeatedly proved by the most incontrovertible facts in our literature, namely, that the new *Iskra*-ists represent the opportunist, and their opponents the revolutionary, wing of contemporary Russian Social-Democracy. The Liberals cannot help sympathising with the tendencies of the former and censuring the tendencies of the latter. Being the ideologists of the bourgeoisie, the Liberals fully understand the advantages ensuing to the bourgeoisie from the "practicalness, sobriety, and serious-mindedness" of the working class, *i.e.*, its practically confining its activities within the limits of capitalism, reforms, trade union struggle, etc. What is dangerous and terrible to the bourgeoisie is the "revolutionary narrow-mindedness" of the proletariat and its striving to obtain, in order to achieve its class aims, a leading rôle in the all-national Russian revolution.

That this is the real meaning of the word "realism" in its *Osvobozhdeniye* sense, is evident, among other things, from the way it was used formerly by *Osvobozhdeniye* and by Mr. Struve. *Iskra* itself had to admit that this was the meaning of *Osvobozhdeniye* "realism." Recall to your mind, for instance, the article, "It is High Time!" in the supplement to *Iskra*, No. 73-74. The author of this article (a consistent interpreter of the views held by the "swamp" at the Second Congress of the Russian Social-Democratic Labour Party) frankly expressed the opinion that "at the Congress Akimov played the part of the spectre of opportunism, rather than of its real representative" and the Editorial Board of *Iskra* was immediately obliged to correct the author of the article, "It is High Time!" and state in a note:

We cannot agree with this view. Comrade Akimov's programme bears the clear imprint of opportunism, and this is admitted even by the *Osvobozhdeniye* critic who, in one of its recent issues, stated that Comrade Akimov is an adherent of the "realist," in other words, revisionist, tendency.

Thus *Iskra* itself is perfectly well aware that "realism" in the *Osvobozhdeniye* sense is simply opportunism and nothing else. Now in attacking "liberal realism" (*Iskra*, No. 102) *Iskra* quietly ignores the fact that *the Liberals praised it* for its realism, and this silence is explained by the fact that such praise is more insulting than any abuse. Such praise (which *Osvobozhdeniye* uttered not by mere chance and not for the first time) proves the affinity that exists between liberal realism and those tendencies of Social-Democratic "realism" (in other words, opportunism) which manifest themselves in every resolution adopted by the new *Iskra*-ists, owing to the error of their whole tactical line.

Indeed the Russian bourgeoisie has already fully revealed its inconsistency and selfishness in the "all-national" revolution—it has revealed it in Mr. Struve's arguments and by the whole tone and content of a large number of liberal papers, by the character of the political utterances of many Zemstvoists, intellectuals, and of all the adherents of Messrs. Trubetskoy, Petrunkevich, Rodichev and Co. Generally the bourgeoisie does not, of course, always clearly understand, but on the whole it excellently realises by its class instinct that on the one hand, the proletariat and the "people" can serve *its* revolution as cannon-fodder, as a battering-ram against the autocracy, but that, on the other hand, the proletariat and the revolutionary peasantry will be terribly dangerous to it if they win a "decisive victory over tsarism" and carry the democratic revolution to its end. Therefore, the bourgeoisie tries its utmost to make the proletariat satisfied with a "modest" rôle in the revolution, so as to render it more sober, practical and realistic, so that its activity might be circumscribed by the principle "lest the bourgeoisie desert."

The enlightened bourgeoisie is perfectly well aware that it will not be able to get rid of the labour movement. Hence, it does not oppose the labour movement, or the proletarian class struggle—no, it even pays lip service to the right to strike and to wage a cultured class struggle, it conceives the labour movement and the class struggle in the Brentano and Hirsch-Dunker * sense. In other words, it is fully prepared to "yield" to the workers the right to strike and to organise in trade unions (which have already almost been won by the workers themselves), provided the workers give up their "rebelliousness," their "narrow-minded revolutionism," their hostility to "practical and useful compromises," their claims and aspirations to lay the imprint of *their* class struggle on the "All-National Russian Revolution," the imprint of proletarian consistency, of proletarian determination, and of "plebeian Jacobinism." That is why the enlightened bourgeoisie all over Russia, by thousands of ways and means—books,** lectures, speeches, talks, etc., etc.—tries with all its might to instil into the minds of the workers the ideas of (bourgeois) sobriety, of (liberal) practicability, of (opportunist) realism, of (Brentano) class struggle, of (Hirsch-Dunker) trade unions, etc. The two last named slogans are particularly convenient for the

---

* Lujo Brentano was a prominent professor and "socialist of the chair"— the German counter-part of Russian "Legal Marxism" (see note 15)—who preached class harmony. The Hirsch-Dunker labor unions, favoring a class-collaboration policy, were formed in opposition to the unions led by the early German socialists.—*Ed.*

** *Cf.* Prokopovitch, *The Labour Question in Russia.*

bourgeoisie of the "Constitutional-Democratic" or *Osvobozhdeniye* parties, for outwardly they coincide with the Marxist slogans, and after being a little curtailed and distorted they can easily be made to look like the Social-Democratic slogans, and sometimes even be passed off for the latter. For example, the legal, liberal paper *Rassvyet* * (which we shall discuss with the readers of *Proletary* in greater detail another time) often expresses such "bold" ideas on class struggle, on the possibility that the bourgeoisie will deceive the proletariat, on the labour movement, on the self-activity of the proletariat, etc., etc., that an inattentive reader and an unenlightened worker might easily be led to believe that its "social-democracy" was genuine. In fact, however, it is a bourgeois imitation of Social-Democracy, an opportunist perversion and distortion of the concept of the class struggle.

At the root of this gigantic (as regards the extent of its influence over the masses) bourgeois subterfuge lies the tendency to confine the labour movement mainly to the trade union movement, to keep it away as far as possible from adopting an independent policy (*i.e.*, revolutionary policy tending towards the democratic dictatorship), to "obscure in the workers' minds the idea of an all-national Russian revolution by the idea of class struggle."

As the reader will perceive, we have turned the *Osvobozhdeniye* formula upside down. This is an excellent formula which fully expresses the two views held on the rôle of the proletariat in the democratic revolution, the bourgeois view and the Social-Democratic view. The bourgeoisie wishes to confine the proletariat exclusively to the trade union movement and thereby "obscure in the workers' minds the idea of an all-national Russian revolution by the idea of the (Brentano) class struggle"—which is entirely in keeping with the Bernsteinist authors of the *Credo* who in the minds of the workers obscured the idea of the political struggle by the idea of a "pure labour" movement. Social-Democracy, on the contrary, wishes to develop the proletarian class struggle so that it can take a leading part in an all-national Russian revolution, *i.e.*, to lead this revolution to the democratic dictatorship of the proletariat and the peasantry

Our revolution is all-national, says the bourgeoisie to the proletariat. Therefore, you, being a separate class, must confine yourselves to your class struggle, and in the name of "common sense" must direct your attention mainly to the trade unions and on getting

* *The Dawn.—Ed.*

them legalised, you must regard precisely these trade unions as "the most important starting point for your political education and organisation"—in a revolutionary situation you must concern yourselves mainly with drawing up "serious" resolutions like the one adopted by new *Iskra*, you must treat resolutions which are "more favourable to the liberals," with greatest care, you must prefer leaders who display a tendency to become "practical leaders of a real political, working-class movement," you must "preserve the realist elements of the Marxist philosophy" (if unfortunately you have become infected with the "strict formulae" of this "unscientific" catechism).

Our revolution is all-national, says the Social-Democracy to the proletariat. Therefore, you, as the most advanced revolutionary class, the only class that is consistent to the end, must strive not only to take a very energetic but also a leading part in the revolution. Therefore, you must not confine yourselves to the narrow conception of the scope of the class struggle, *i.e.*, mainly as a trade union movement, but, on the contrary, you must strive to widen the scope and content of your class struggle, so as *to include* not only *all* the tasks of the real, democratic, all-national Russian revolution, but also the tasks of the subsequent socialist revolution. Therefore, without ignoring the trade union movement, without refusing to make use even of the slightest legal possibilities, you must, in a time of revolution, bring to the fore the tasks of the armed uprising, of forming a revolutionary army and revolutionary government, which is the only road to the complete victory of the people over tsarism, to the achievement of a democratic republic and of real political liberty.

It is superfluous to add that owing to their erroneous "line," the new *Iskra* resolutions take up a very half-hearted and inconsistent position on this question, naturally sympathetic towards the bourgeoisie.

II. COMRADE MARTYNOV ONCE MORE "DEEPENS" THE QUESTION

Let us pass on to Martynov's articles in the *Iskra*, Nos. 102 and 103. Of course, we shall not reply to Martynov's attempts to prove that we are wrong and he is right in the interpretation of a number of quotations from Engels and Marx. These attempts are so frivolous, his subterfuges are so obvious, the question is so clear, that there would be no interest in dwelling on this once more. Every thinking reader will easily be able to see through the naïve devices to which Martynov resorts in his retreat along the whole line, especially after the complete translations of Engels' pamphlet, *The Bakuninists at Work*, and Marx's, *Manifesto of the Council of the Communist League*, of March, 1850, now being prepared by a group of collaborators of the *Proletary*, are published. One quotation from Martynov's article will suffice to make this retreat clear to the reader.

Martynov says in No. 103:

> *Iskra* admits that the establishment of a provisional government is one of the possible and expedient ways of the development of the revolution and denies the expediency of Social-Democrats participating in a *bourgeois* provisional government, precisely in order that the state apparatus may be completely captured for the social-democratic revolution in the future.

In other words, *Iskra* now admits the absurdity of its fears concerning the responsibility which a revolutionary government will have to bear for the exchequer and the banks, the danger and the impossibility of taking over "prisons," etc. But *Iskra* is blundering as before and is still confusing the democratic dictatorship with the socialist dictatorship. This muddle is inevitable, as a cover for retreat.

However, among the muddle-heads of new *Iskra*, Martynov stands out as a muddle-head of first rank, as a muddle-head of talent, if we may say so. Confusing the question by his vain efforts to "deepen" it, he almost always "thinks out" new formulae, which magnificently reveal the fallacy of his position. You will remember how in the days of Economism he "deepened" Plekhanov and creatively produced a new formula, "economic struggle against the employers and the government." It is difficult to find in the whole literature of the Economists a better expression of the fallacy of Economism. We see the same thing today. Martynov zealously serves the new *Iskra*, and almost every time he speaks, he gives us new and excellent material for evaluating the false position of new *Iskra*. In No. 102 he stated that Lenin "has imperceptibly substituted the concept dictatorship for revolution." (P. 3, column 2.)

As a matter of fact, all the accusations which the new *Iskra*-ists hurl against us can be reduced to this. And how grateful we are to Martynov for this accusation! What an invaluable service he renders us in the cause of our struggle against new *Iskra*-ism by formulating his accusation in this way! We must positively beg the editors of *Iskra* to set Martynov against us as often as possible in order to "deepen" the attacks on *Proletary* and in order to formulate them in accordance with "true principles." Because the more Martynov tries to argue in accordance with strict principles, the more he fails, the more clearly he reveals the rents in new *Iskra*-ism, and the more successfully does he perform on himself and his friends the useful pedagogical operation, *viz., reductio ad absurdum* of the new *Iskra* principles.

Vperyod and *Proletary* "substitute" the concept dictatorship for revolution; *Iskra* does not want such a "substitute." Just so, most esteemed Comrade Martynov! Accidentally you blurted out a great truth. Your *new* formula confirms our proposition that *Iskra* is dragging at the tail of the revolution, is being sidetracked to the *Osvobozhdeniye*-ist formulation of its tasks, whereas *Vperyod* and *Proletary* issue slogans which lead the democratic revolution onward.

You don't understand this, Comrade Martynov? In view of the importance of the question, we shall try to give you a detailed explanation.

The bourgeois character of the democratic revolution is expressed, among other things, by the fact that a number of social classes, groups and strata, which fully recognise the principles of private property and commodity production, and which are incapable of going beyond these limits, are nevertheless forced by circumstances to recognise the worthlessness of autocracy and of the whole feudal regime in general, and join in the demand for freedom. And in this connection the bourgeois character of *this* freedom which is demanded by "society," and advocated in a flood of words (and only words!) by landlords and capitalists, is manifesting itself more and more clearly. At the same time, the fundamental difference between the workers' struggle for freedom and that of the bourgeoisie, between proletarian and liberal democracy, becomes more and more obvious. The working class and its class-conscious representatives are marching onward and are advancing this struggle; they are not only not afraid to carry it to the end, but aspire to do so far beyond the farthest limits of the democratic revolution. The bourgeoisie is inconsistent and selfish and accepts the slogans of freedom only incompletely and hypocritically. All attempts to draw a line, or to define by specially formulated "points" (like the points of the Starover resolution, or of the Conference-makers) the limits beyond which begins the hypocrisy of the bourgeois friends of freedom, or, if you like, the betrayal of liberty by its bourgeois friends, are inevitably doomed to failure, for the bourgeoisie, placed between two fires (the autocracy and the proletariat), is by a thousand ways and means capable of changing its position and slogans, of adapting itself just an inch to the left or an inch to the right, always bargaining and haggling like a broker. The task of proletarian democracy is not to invent such sterile "points," but to unceasingly criticise the developing political situation, to expose the new unforeseen inconsistencies and acts of treachery of the bourgeoisie.

Recall the history of Mr. Struve's political writings in the illegal press, the history of the war Social-Democracy waged against him, and you will clearly see how these were developed by Social-Democracy, the champion of proletarian democracy. Mr. Struve began with a purely Shipov slogan: *"Rights and Zemstvos vested with power"* (see my article in the *Zarya*, "The Persecutors of the Zemstvo and the Hannibals of Liberalism"). Social-Democracy exposed him and was pushing him towards a definitely constitutional programme. When this "pushing" took effect owing to the specially rapid development of revolutionary events, the struggle was transferred to the *next* question of democracy: not only a constitution in general, but universal, direct and equal suffrage with secret ballot. When we "captured" this new position from the "enemy" (the adoption of universal suffrage by the Emancipation [*Osvobozhdeniye*] League), we pressed further forward and exposed the hypocrisy and falsity of the two chamber system, we proved that the *Osvobozhdeniye*-ists did not entirely accept universal suffrage, and pointing to their *monarchism*, we exposed the stock-jobbing character of their democracy, or, in other words, the *bargaining away* of the interests of the great Russian Revolution by these *Osvobozhdeniye* money-bag heroes.

Finally, the savage obstinacy of autocracy, the gigantic progress of the civil war, the hopelessness of the condition to which the monarchists have reduced Russia have begun to penetrate even the thickest skulls. Revolution has become an actual *fact*. It was no longer necessary to be a revolutionary to recognise revolution. The autocratic government practically was falling and is falling to pieces in the sight of all. As a certain liberal (Mr. Gredeskul) has justly remarked in the legal press, this government is practically not being obeyed. In spite of its apparent strength, the autocracy has proved to be impotent; the events of the developing revolution are simply pushing aside this parasitical organism which is decaying alive.

Compelled to base their activity (or rather their political wire-pulling) on the relationships actually being created, the liberal bourgeois *have begun to realise the necessity of recognising the revolution.* They do this not because they are revolutionaries, but in spite of the fact that they are not revolutionaries. They do so of necessity and against their will, viewing the successes of the revolution with an angry eye, accusing the autocracy of being revolutionary, because it does not want to strike a bargain but wants a life and death struggle instead. Born hucksters as they are, they hate the struggle and the revolution, but circumstances force them to tread the ground of the revolution, for there is no other ground under their feet.

We are witnessing a highly instructive and highly comical spectacle. The prostitutes of bourgeois liberalism are trying to don the mantle of revolutionism. The *Osvobozhdeniye*-ists—*risum teneatis, amici!* *—are beginning to speak in the name of the revolution! The *Osvobozhdeniye*-ists are beginning to assure us that they are "not afraid of the revolution" (Mr. Struve in *Osvobozhdeniye*, No. 72)!!! The *Osvobozhdeniye*-ists are putting forth the claim to "put themselves at the head of the revolution!!"

This is a very significant phenomenon, which not only characterises the progress of bourgeois liberalism, but still more the progress of the real successes of the revolutionary movement, which *compelled* recognition for itself. Even the bourgeoisie is beginning to realise that it is more advantageous to take its stand by revolution—to such an extent has the autocracy been shaken. On the other hand, this phenomenon indicates that the whole movement has risen to a new and higher plane, and therefore confronts us with equally new and higher tasks. The recognition of the revolution on the part of the bourgeoisie cannot be sincere, apart from the personal integrity of this or that bourgeois ideologist. The bourgeoisie cannot help introducing selfishness and inconsistency, huckstering and petty reactionary subterfuges even into this higher stage of the movement. We must now formulate *differently* the immediate *concrete* tasks of the revolution in the name of our programme and in the development of our programme. What was adequate yesterday is *inadequate today.* Yesterday, perhaps, the demand for the recognition of the revolution was sufficient to serve as a progressive democratic slogan. Now it is not enough. The revolution has forced even Mr. Struve

* Restrain your laughter, friends!—*Ed.*

to recognise it. The advanced class must now define precisely the *very content* of the pressing and urgent tasks of this revolution. While recognising the revolution, Messrs. Struve again and again expose their asinine ears when they sing their old song about the possibility of a peaceful issue, of *Nicholas* inviting messieurs the *Osvobozhdeniye*-ists to assume the government, etc., etc. Messieurs the *Osvobozhdeniye*-ists recognise the revolution in order to cheat the revolution, to betray it in the safest possible manner for themselves. Our business now is to show the proletariat and the whole people the inadequacy of the slogan, "revolution," to show the necessity of a clear and unambiguous, consistent and decisive definition of the *very content* of the revolution. And this definition is provided by the slogan which alone is capable of expressing correctly the "decisive victory" of the revolution, *viz.*, the slogan of the revolutionary democratic dictatorship of the proletariat and the peasantry.

We have shown that the *Osvobozhdeniye*-ists are ascending (not without the influence of encouraging pushes from Social-Democracy) step by step in the matter of recognising democracy. At first the issue in the dispute between them and ourselves was: the Shipov system (rights and Zemstvos vested with power) or constitutionalism? Then, limited or universal suffrage? Further the recognition of the revolution or a stock-jobbing deal with autocracy? Finally, at the present time: the recognition of the revolution without the dictatorship of the proletariat and the peasantry or the recognition of the demand for the dictatorship of these classes in a democratic revolution. It is possible and probable that the *Osvobozhdeniye*-ists too (it does not matter whether the present ones or their successors in the Left wing of bourgeois democracy) will ascend another step, *i.e.*, will in time recognise (perhaps by the time Comrade Martynov ascends another step) the slogan of dictatorship. It is even bound to happen, if the Russian revolution will advance successfully and result in a decisive victory. What will then be the position of Social-Democracy? A complete victory of the present revolution will be the end of the democratic revolution and the beginning of a decisive struggle for the socialist revolution. The realisation of the demands of the present-day peasantry, the complete rout of the reaction, the conquest of a democratic republic, will mark the end of the revolutionism of the bourgeoisie and even of the petty-bourgeoisie—it will be the beginning of a real proletarian struggle for socialism. The more complete the democratic revolution will be, the sooner, the wider, the purer, and the more resolutely will this new struggle develop. The slogan, "democratic" dictatorship, expresses precisely the historically limited character of the present revolution and the necessity of a new struggle on the basis of a new order, for the complete emancipation of the working class from all oppression and all exploitation. In other words, when the democratic bourgeoisie or the petty-bourgeoisie ascends another step, when not only the revolution but the complete victory of the revolution will have become a fact, we shall "substitute" (perhaps amidst the terrible wailing of some future Martynovs) for the slogan, the democratic dictatorship, the slogan, the socialist dictatorship of the proletariat, *i.e.*, complete socialist revolution.

III. THE VULGAR BOURGEOIS REPRESENTATION OF DICTATORSHIP AND MARX'S VIEWS ON DICTATORSHIP

Mehring tells us in his notes to his edition of Marx's articles from *Die Neue Rheinische Zeitung* of 1848 that incidentally the following reproach was hurled at this newspaper in the bourgeois publications. *Die Neue Rheinische Zeitung* was alleged to have demanded "the immediate introduction of a dictatorship as the only means of achieving democracy." (Marx, *Nachlass*, Vol. III, p. 53.) From the vulgar bourgeois standpoint the concepts dictatorship and democracy mutually exclude each other. Not understanding the theory of class struggle and accustomed to seeing in the political arena only a petty squabble of various bourgeois circles and cliques, the bourgeois conceives the dictatorship to be the repeal of all liberties, of all guarantees of democracy, tyranny of every kind and all possible abuses of power in the personal interests of the dictator. In effect, it is precisely this vulgar-bourgeois viewpoint that permeates the writings of our Martynov, who winds up his "new campaign" in the new *Iskra* by attributing the partiality of *Vperyod* and *Proletary* to the slogan of dictatorship to Lenin's "being obsessed by a passionate desire to try his luck." (*Iskra*, No. 103, p. 3, column 2.) In order to explain to Martynov the concept of class dictatorship as distinguished from personal dictatorship and the tasks of democratic dictatorship as distinguished from socialist dictatorship, it would be useful to dwell on the views of *Die Neue Rheinische Zeitung*.

On September 14, 1848, *Die Neue Rheinische Zeitung* wrote:

After a revolution, every provisional organisation of the state requires a dictatorship, and an energetic dictatorship at that. From the very beginning we have reproached Kamphausen [the head of the ministry after March 18, 1848] for not acting dictatorially, for not having immediately smashed up and eliminated the remnants of old institutions. And while Mr. Kamphausen was thus rocking himself in constitutional dreams the defeated party (*i.e.*, the party of reaction) strengthened its positions in the bureaucracy and in the army, and here and there even began to venture upon open struggle.

These few words, Mehring justly remarks, sum up in a few propositions all that was propounded by *Die Neue Rheinische Zeitung* in long articles on Kamphausen's ministry. What do these words of Marx imply? That the provisional revolutionary government *must* act dictatorially (a proposition which *Iskra* was altogether unable to grasp since it was fighting shy of the slogan, dictatorship), that the task of such a dictatorship is to destroy the remnants of old institutions (precisely what was clearly indicated in the resolution of the Third Congress of the Russian Social-Democratic Labour Party on the struggle against the counter-revolution and which, as we have indicated above, was omitted in the resolution of the Conference). Thirdly, and finally, it follows from these words that Marx castigated the bourgeois democrats for entertaining "constitutional dreams" in an epoch of revolution and open civil war. The meaning of these words becomes particularly obvious from the article in *Die Neue Rheinische Zeitung* of June 6, 1848. Marx wrote:

A constituent national assembly must first of all be an active, revolutionary-active assembly. But the Frankfort Assembly is busying itself with school exercises in parliamentarism while allowing the government to act. Let us assume that this learned assembly succeeded after mature consideration in working out the best agenda and the best constitution. But what would be the use of the best agenda and of the best constitution, if the government had in the meantime placed the bayonet on the agenda?

Such is the meaning of the slogan, dictatorship. Hence we can gauge what Marx's attitude would have been towards resolutions which call the "decision to organise a constituent assembly" a decisive victory or which invite us to "remain a party of extreme revolutionary opposition."

Great questions in the life of nations are settled only by force. The reactionary classes are usually themselves the first to resort to violence, to civil war; they are the first to "place the bayonet on the agenda," as Russian autocracy has been doing systematically, consistently, everywhere, all over the country, ever since January 22[9]. And since such a situation has arisen, since the bayonet has really taken first place on the political agenda, since the uprising has become necessary and urgent—the constitutional dreams and school exercises in parliamentarism are becoming only a screen for the bourgeois betrayal of the revolution, a screen for the "desertion" of the bourgeoisie from the cause of the revolution. The genuinely revolutionary class must, then, advance precisely the slogan of dictatorship.

On the question of the tasks of this dictatorship Marx had already written in *Die Neue Rheinische Zeitung* as follows:

> The national assembly should have acted dictatorially against all the reactionary attempts of the obsolete governments and then it would have gained on its side public opinion of such power against which all bayonets and rifle butts would have broken into splinters.... But this assembly bores the German people instead of carrying the people with it or being carried away by it.

In the opinion of Marx, the national assembly should have "eliminated from the actually existing regime of Germany everything that contradicted the principle of the sovereignty of the people," then "it should have defended the revolutionary ground on which it rested in order to make the sovereignty of the people, won by the revolution, secure against all attacks."

Thus, the tasks which Marx set before the revolutionary government or the dictatorship in 1848 amounted in substance first of all to *democratic* revolution, *i.e.*, defence against counter-revolution and actual abolition of everything that contradicted the sovereignty of the people. And this is nothing else than revolutionary-democratic dictatorship.

To proceed: which were the classes that in the opinion of Marx could have and should have achieved that task (to carry into effect the principle of the people's sovereignty to the end and to beat off the attacks of the counter-revolution)? Marx talks of the "people." However, we know that he always ruthlessly combated the petty-bourgeois illusions about the unity of the "people" and about the absence of class struggle among the people. In using the word "people," Marx did not thereby gloss over the class differences, but united certain elements which were capable of carrying the revolution to the end.

After the victory of the Berlin proletariat on March 18, wrote *Die Neue Rheinische Zeitung*, the results of the revolution turned out to be twofold:

> On the one hand the arming of the people, the right of association, the sovereignty of the people actually won; on the other hand, the preservation of the

monarchy and the ministry of Kamphausen-Hansemann, *i.e.*, the government of the representatives of the upper bourgeoisie. Thus the results of the revolution have been twofold and inevitably had to lead to a rupture. The people have emerged victorious; they have won liberties of a decisively democratic nature, but direct power has been transferred not to their hands but to those of the upper bourgeoisie. In a word, the revolution has not been completed. The people allowed the formation of a ministry of the big bourgeois, and the upper bourgeois betrayed their objectives immediately by offering an alliance to the old Prussian nobility and bureaucracy. Arnim, Canitz and Schwerin have joined the Cabinet.

The upper bourgeoisie, anti-revolutionary from the very beginning, has concluded a defensive and offensive alliance with reaction out of fear of the people, that is to say, the workers and the democratic bourgeoisie. (Italics ours.)

Thus, not only a "decision to organise a constituent assembly," but even its actual convocation is insufficient for a decisive victory of the revolution! Even after a partial victory in an armed struggle (the victory of the Berlin workers over the troops on March 18, 1848) an "incomplete" and "unfinished" revolution is possible. What does its final consummation depend on? It depends on the question: To whose hands is the immediate rule transferred? To those of the Petrunkeviches or Rodichevs,* that is to say, the Kamphausens and the Hansemanns, or of the *people, i.e.*, of the workers and the democratic bourgeoisie? In the first case the bourgeoisie will possess power, and the proletariat—"freedom to criticise," freedom to "remain a party of extreme revolutionary opposition." Immediately after victory the bourgeoisie will enter into an alliance with reaction (this would also inevitably happen in Russia, if, for example, the St. Petersburg workers gained only a partial victory in a street fight with the troops and allowed Messrs. Petrunkevich and Co. to form a government). In the second case a revolutionary-democratic dictatorship, *i.e.*, a complete victory of the revolution, would be possible.

It remains to define more precisely what Marx really meant by "democratic bourgeoisie" (*demokratische Bürgerschaft*), which together with the workers he called the people, in contradistinction to the big bourgeoisie.

A clear answer to this question is supplied by the following passage in the article in *Die Neue Rheinische Zeitung* of July 29, 1848:

...the German revolution of 1848 is only a parody of the French revolution of 1789.

On August 4, 1789, three weeks after the storming of the Bastille, the French people in a single day prevailed over all the feudal services.

* Leaders of the Constitutional-Democratic Party in Russia.—*Ed.*

113

On July 11, 1848, four months after the March barricades, the feudal services prevailed over the German people. *Teste Gierke cum Hansemanno.**

The French bourgeoisie of 1789 did not for a moment abandon its allies, the peasants. It knew that its rule was based on the destruction of feudalism in the villages, the creation of a free landowning (*grundbesitzenden*) peasant class.

The German bourgeoisie of 1848 is, without the least compunction, betraying the peasants, its most natural allies, who are flesh of its flesh, and without whom it is powerless as against the nobility.

The preservation of feudal rights, their sanction under the guise of (illusory) compensation—such is the result of the German revolution of 1848. The mountain has brought forth a mouse.

This is a very instructive passage which gives us four important propositions: (1) the incomplete German revolution differs from the complete French revolution in that the German bourgeoisie betrayed not only democracy in general, but in particular the peasantry as well. (2) The foundation for the complete accomplishment of a democratic revolution is the creation of a free class of peasants. (3) The creation of such a class means the abolition of feudal services, the destruction of feudalism, but does not yet mean a socialist revolution. (4) The peasants are the "most natural" allies of the bourgeoisie, that is to say, the democratic bourgeoisie, without whom it is "powerless" against reaction.

Making corresponding allowances for the concrete national peculiarities and substituting serfdom in place of feudalism, all these propositions will be fully applicable to Russia of 1905. There is no doubt that by learning from the experience of Germany, as elucidated by Marx, we cannot adopt any other slogan for a decisive victory of the revolution than the revolutionary-democratic dictatorship of the proletariat and the peasantry. There is no doubt that the main constituent parts of the "people," whom Marx in 1848 contrasted with the resisting reaction and the treacherous bourgeoisie, are the proletariat and the peasantry. Undoubtedly, in Russia too, the liberal bourgeoisie and the gentlemen of *Osvobozhdeniye* are betraying and will betray the peasantry, *i.e.,* they will confine themselves to a

---

* "Witnesses to this are Gierke and Hansemann." Hansemann was the minister of the party of the big bourgeoisie (like Trubetskoy or Rodichev, etc., in Russia), Gierke was the minister of agriculture in the Hansemann Cabinet, who worked out a bold project for "abolishing feudal services," professedly "without compensation," but which in fact abolished only the minor and unimportant services while preserving or granting compensation for the more substantial ones. Mr. Gierke was somewhat like the Russian Messrs. Kablukovs, Manuilovs, Hertzensteins and similar bourgeois-liberal friends of the muzhik who desire the "extension of peasant landownership" but do not wish to offend the landlords.

pseudo-reform and will take the side of the landlords in the decisive struggle between them and the peasantry. Only the proletariat is capable of supporting the peasantry to the end in this struggle. There is no doubt, finally, that in Russia the success of the peasant struggle, *i.e.*, the transfer of the whole of the land to the peasantry, will signify a complete democratic revolution and form the social support of the revolution carried to its end, but it will by no means signify a socialist revolution, or "socialisation," which is talked about by the ideologists of the petty bourgeoisie, the Socialist-Revolutionaries. The success of the peasant uprising, the victory of the democratic revolution will but clear the way for a genuine and decisive struggle for socialism on the basis of a democratic republic. In this struggle the peasantry as a landowning class will play the same treacherous, vacillating part as that played at present by the bourgeoisie in its struggle for democracy. To forget this means forgetting socialism, deluding oneself and deceiving others with regard to the real interests and tasks of the proletariat.

In order not to leave any gaps in the presentation of the views held by Marx in 1848, it is necessary to note one substantial difference between German Social-Democracy of that time (or the Communist Party of the Proletariat, as it was called) and present-day Russian Social-Democracy. Let us quote Mehring:

Die Neue Rheinische Zeitung appeared in the political arena as the organ of democracy. And although an unmistakably red thread ran through all its articles, it directly defended the interests of the bourgeois revolution against absolutism and feudalism more than the interests of the proletariat against the bourgeoisie. You will find very little material in its columns about the separate labour movement during the revolution, although one should not forget that along with it there appeared twice a week, under the editorship of Moll and Schapper, a special organ of the Cologne Labour League. In any case the reader of today will immediately notice how slight was the attention paid by *Die Neue Rheinische Zeitung* to the German labour movement of its day, although its most capable representative, Stephan Born, was a pupil of Marx and Engels in Paris and Brussels and in 1848 wrote to their newspaper from Berlin. Born mentions in his memoirs that Marx and Engels never in the slightest degree expressed their disapproval of his agitation among the workers. But the subsequent declarations of Engels render probable the supposition that they were dissatisfied, at least with the methods of this agitation. Their dissatisfaction was well founded in so far as Born was forced to make many concessions to the proletariat whose class-consciousness was as yet entirely undeveloped in the greater part of Germany, concessions which could not stand the test of criticism if viewed from the standpoint of the *Communist Manifesto*. Their dissatisfaction was unfounded in so far as Born managed none the less to maintain the agitation conducted by him on a relatively high plane.... No doubt Marx and Engels were historically and politically right when they thought that the working class was above all interested in pushing the bourgeois revolution as far as possible.... Nevertheless, remarkable proof of how the elementary instinct of the labour movement is able to correct the conceptions of the most brilliant thinkers is provided by the fact that, in April, 1849, they expressed themselves in favour of a specific workers' organisation and of participation in the labour congress, which was being prepared especially by the East Elba [East Prussia] proletariat.

Thus, it was only in April, 1849, after the revolutionary newspaper had been published for almost a year (*Die Neue Rheinische Zeitung* made its first appearance on June 1, 1848) that Marx and Engels declared themselves in favour of a special workers' organisation! Until then they were merely running an "organ of democracy" unconnected by any organisational ties with an independent workers' party. This fact, monstrous and incredible from our present-day standpoint, clearly shows us what an enormous difference there is between the German workers' party of those days and the present Russian Social-Democratic Labour Party. This fact shows also how much less the proletarian features of the movement, its proletarian current, were in evidence in the German democratic revolution (because of the backwardness of Germany in 1848 both in the economic and the political fields, and the political disintegration of the country). This should not be forgotten in evaluating the declarations Marx repeatedly made during this period and a little later about the need for independently organising a proletarian party. Marx drew this practical conclusion only as a result of the experience of the democratic revolution almost a year later, so philistine and petty-bourgeois was the whole atmosphere in Germany then. This conclusion is to us an old and solid acquisition of half a century's experience of international Social-Democracy—an acquisition with which we began to organise the Russian Social-Democratic Labour Party. In our case it is absolutely impossible for revolutionary proletarian papers to keep outside the pale of the Social-Democratic Party of the proletariat, or for them to appear even once simply as "organs of democracy."

But the contrast which only began to reveal itself between Marx and Stephan Born exists in our case in a form which is the more developed, the more powerfully the proletarian current manifests itself in the democratic stream of our revolution. Speaking of the probable dissatisfaction of Marx and Engels with the agitation conducted by Stephan Born, Mehring expresses himself too mildly and too evasively. This is what Engels wrote about Born in 1885 (in the preface to the *Enthüllungen über den Kommunistenprozess zu Köln,** Zürich, 1885) :

The members of the Communist League stood everywhere at the head of the extreme democratic movement, proving thereby that the League was an excellent school of revolutionary activity. Stephan Born, a compositor, who was an active member of the League in Brussels and Paris, founded a "Workers' Brotherhood" (*Arbeiter Verbrüderung*) in Berlin which had a considerable following and lasted until 1850. Born, a highly talented young man, was, however, in too great a hurry to come forward as a public man. He "fraternised" with a very motley crew (Kreti and Plethi), in order to gather a crowd of people around himself. He was by no means the man to introduce unity into discordant tendencies, to bring light into chaos. Therefore, in the official publications of this Brotherhood one constantly came across a muddle and a confusion of the views of the *Communist Manifesto* with guild reminiscences and aspirations, with fragments of the views of Louis Blanc and Proudhon, with an apology for protectionism, etc.—in fine, these people wanted to be all things to all men (*Allen Alles sein*). *They were especially engaged in organising strikes, trade unions, producers' associations, forgetting that first of all it was necessary by means of political victories to win the ground upon which alone such things may be made durable.* [Italics ours.] And when the victories of reaction forced the leaders of this Brotherhood to realise the need for taking a direct part in the revolutionary struggle, they were, of course, deserted by the confused masses, which had hitherto surrounded them. Born took part in the Dresden uprising in May, 1849, and had a lucky escape. The Workers' Brotherhood, on the other hand, kept aloof from the great political movement of the proletariat as an isolated body which existed mainly on paper and which played such a secondary role that the reaction deemed it necessary to close it only in 1850, and its branches even several years later. Born, whose real name was Buttermilch ** [Buttermilk] did not after all become a public man, but became an unimportant Swiss professor, who instead of translating Marx into guild language is translating the kind-hearted Renan into sentimental German.

That is how Engels appraised the two tactics of Social-Democracy in the democratic revolution!

Our new *Iskra*-ists are also bent on Economism, and with such unreasonable zeal as to earn the praises of the monarchist bourgeoisie for their "enlightenment." They too collect around themselves a

* *Revelations About the Trial of the Communists at Cologne.—Ed.*
** Born's real name is Buttermilch. In translating Engels I made an error in the first edition in taking the word "Buttermilch," not as a proper but as a generic name. The Mensheviks, naturally, were highly delighted at this error. Kolzov wrote that I had "deepened Engels" (reprinted in the collection, *In Two Years*), Plekhanov also recalls this error in *Tovarisch* (*Comrade*)—in a word, it offered an *excellent pretext to conceal the question of the two tendencies in the working class movement* in 1848 in Germany, the tendency of Born (a relative of our Economists) and the Marxist tendency. To make use of the mistake of an opponent, even if it is on account of Born's name, is quite natural. But to conceal the essence of the question of two tactics by correction of the translation is to surrender the basis of the argument. (Author's note to the 1908 edition.—*Ed.*)

117

motley crowd, by flattering the Economists, by demagogically attracting the unconscious masses by the slogans of "self-activity," "democracy," "autonomy," etc., etc. Their labour unions, too, often exist only on the pages of the braggart new *Iskra*. Their slogans and resolution display an equal lack of comprehension of the tasks of the "great political movement of the proletariat."

July-August, 1905.

EXPLANATORY NOTES

1. The mutiny on the cruiser *Potemkin* suddenly broke out in June 1905, as a result of the high-handed and provocative conduct of the officers who threatened to shoot down the sailors when they refused to eat the putrid meat served out to them. The mutineers, headed by the sailor Matyushenko, a Social-Democrat, disarmed and killed the officers and then issued a manifesto *To the Civilised World* which contained the slogans: "Down with the Autocracy! Long Live the Constituent Assembly!" The *Potemkin* was joined by three other warships and the revolutionary flotilla made its way to Odessa "to protect the revolutionary people." Arriving at Odessa at the time of the strike the crew of the *Potemkin* established contact with the workers and the local revolutionary organizations, but it was very indecisive in its actions. After the treachery of one of the rebel ships and the arrival of the squadron, the *Potemkin* left Odessa, but was finally forced to surrender to the Rumanian government because of lack of coal and provisions and dissension among the sailors. Part of the crew returned to Russia and threw themselves upon the mercy of the authorities. Three were sentenced to death, 19 to penal servitude and 33 to imprisonment.—p. 9*n*.

2. Lenin here refers to the views on the armed uprising advocated by the Mensheviks, and particularly by Martynov in his pamphlet, *Two Dictatorships*. The Mensheviks denied the need for organisational and technical preparations for the uprising on the grounds that an uprising must occur spontaneously in the process of the development of the struggle and of the revolution, and could not be ordered in advance, just as the revolution in itself could not be ordered in advance. This was the tailist theory of the "uprising-process."—p. 9.

3. The term "Narodnik"—literally, "populist"—was first applied to the social movement of the sixties of the last century, its most characteristic feature being the belief in the possibility of a non-capitalist development of Russia and of attaining socialism without the "sore of proletarianisation" and on the basis of the village commune. For a fuller exposition of the Narodnik theories see the article, "Petty-Bourgeois and Proletarian Socialism," in Lenin's *Selected Works*, Vol. III.—p. 9.

4. The Socialist-Revolutionary Party was formed at the end of 1901 by uniting a number of revolutionary Narodnik groups in Russia and abroad. The theoretical views of the new party were a mixture of populism and revisionist distortions of Marxism. It strove to transform the peasant struggle for land and for the re-division of the land into a movement for declaring the land "national property" and for its equal distribution among the "toilers"; and this the Party called "the socialisation of the land." Lenin exposed the petty-bourgeois nature of the "socialism" of the Socialist-Revolutionaries but

at the same time pointed out that since their activities were directed against the landlords and the landlord aristocracy, they were of positive revolutionary value.—p. 9.

5. The *Iskra* (*Spark*) was founded on Lenin's initiative in 1900 and was edited by him until 1903. At the Second Party Congress in 1903 the *Iskra* became the organ of the Party. The struggle over the composition of the editorial board at this Congress was one of the reasons for the split into a majority (Bolsheviks) and minority (Mensheviks). After the Congress the *Iskra* came under the control of the Mensheviks, following the desertion of Plekhanov to opportunism which led to the resignation of Lenin from the Editorial Board. The paper was now designated by Lenin as the new *Iskra* and its adherents as the new *Iskra*-ists.—p. 11.

6. The reference is to the article, *The Black Sea Mutiny*, by L. Martov printed in *Iskra* (No. 104), in which the author stated that "when the sudden outbreak of the uprising placed a powerful fighting weapon in the hands of the Social-Democrats, they were faced with the task of organising revolution." At the same time, however, he was opposed to the preparatory work of the Social-Democrats in organising a national uprising. "In this uprising," he wrote, "the still prevalent hopes of a universal uprising 'according to plan' proved futile!"—p. 11.

7. The Bulygin Duma, named after the Minister of the Interior at the time, was summoned by the tsar's ukase of August 19 (6), 1905. The Duma was intended to be a purely consultative body made up of representatives of the big landlords and the upper bourgeoisie. The workers were completely excluded from the suffrage, and the peasants were to be weeded out by means of a three-stage system of election. The revolutionary storm which broke out in October swept the Duma away before it had really come into existence.—p. 13.

8. The Constitutional-Democratic Party (known in abbreviated form as Cadets) was the first legal political party of the liberal bourgeoisie in Russia and arose from two groups: the Emancipation League and the Union of Zemstvo Constitutionalists. Lenin often emphasised that the Cadets were a Party of constitutional monarchists. Eventually, at its second congress in 1906, the following point was incorporated in its program: "Russia should be a constitutional, parliamentary monarchy." (See note 19.)—p. 13.

9. The programme of the Russian Social-Democratic Labour Party, adopted at the Second Congress, consisted of two parts: a maximum programme setting forth the ultimate aims (the dictatorship of the proletariat and the building of socialism) and a minimum programme, containing the immediate demands of the proletariat, which could be realized even under capitalism and the purpose of which was to destroy the relics of feudalism and to remove the obstacles to the development of the proletarian class struggle. The minimum programme included such demands as the overthrow of the autocracy, a democratic republic, universal, direct and equal suffrage, secret ballot, freedom of person, press, speech and assembly, the right of nations to self-determination, the eight-hour day, labor protection law, etc. The division of the programme into maximum and minimum was discontinued after the proletariat seized power in Russia and no such division was, of course, made in the new

programme of the Russian Communist Party adopted at the Eighth Party Congress in 1918.—p. 18.

10. Lenin has in mind the Socialist-Revolutionaries who denied the bourgeois character of the 1905 revolution, and also Trotsky and Parvus who held the view that after the overthrow of the autocracy a "labour democratic government, a social-Democratic government" would come into power.—p. 19.

11. In an article entitled, *The Russian Revolution and Peace—An Open Letter to J. Jaurès*, which appeared in *Osvobozhdeniye* [*Emancipation*] in June 1905, Struve wrote: "Speaking theoretically and abstractly, the revolution in Russia may become a government in the most peaceful manner in the world, just as peacefully and simply as a change of ministries takes place in parliamentary countries. . . . Let, for instance, a congress of Zemstvo delegates such as was held in Moscow on May 6 and the following days, meet in Moscow for the space of only two hours. This congress would recommend to Nicholas II the persons needed for a *strong* government, persons who enjoy confidence and prestige in the eyes of the country. And after adopting the programme of these persons, let Nicholas II hand over power to them. For Russia now needs not only freedom, but also an organisation of power that will be able to protect freedom and order."—p. 21.

12. The Frankfort Parliament, "The Frankfort Talking Shop," was the national assembly summoned during the German Revolution of 1848, of which Engels in 1852 in his *Germany: Revolution and Counter-Revolution*, wrote as follows: "This Assembly of old women was, from the first day of its existence, more frightened of the least popular movement than of all the reactionary plots of all the German governments put together. . . . Instead of asserting its own sovereignty, it studiously avoided the discussion of any such dangerous question. Instead of surrounding itself by a popular force, it passed to the order of the day over all the violent encroachments of the government. . . . Thus we had the strange spectacle of an Assembly pretending to be only legal representative of a great and sovereign nation, and yet never possessing either the will or the force to make its claims recognised." This Assembly, continues Engels, "carried away by unequalled cowardice, only restored to their former solidity the foundations upon which the present counter-revolutionary system is built." (Frederick Engels, *Germany: Revolution and Counter-Revolution*, International Publishers, pp. 51, 53.)—p. 24.

13. In addition to this resolution, the Third Congress adopted two other resolutions, not for publication, on the attitude toward the Mensheviks. The resolutions read as follows: (1) "The Third Congress of the R.S.-D.L.P. authorises the Central Committee to take all necessary measures for preparing and drawing up the conditions for fusion with the seceded section of the R.S.-D.L.P., these conditions to be submitted for final approval to the new Party Congress. (2) In view of the possibility that certain of the Menshevik organisations may refuse to accept the decisions of the Third Congress, the Congress instructs the Central Committee to dissolve such organisations and to approve as committees such parallel organisations as submit to the Congress, but only after it shall have been fully established by careful investigation that the Menshevik organisations and committees refuse to submit to Party discipline."—p. 24n.

14. Lenin refers to the demand put forward in the summer of 1905 by the Right wing of the liberal bourgeoisie, headed by D. N. Shipov, for the constitution which, in effect, approximated very closely the plan for a Bulygin Duma (see note 7), for it did not demand universal suffrage, provided for a two chamber system and offered a number of political privileges to the landlords and the bourgeoisie.—p. 28.

15. The "legal Marxists" were bourgeois ideologues who thought they could use Marxism in the class interests of the bourgeoisie. From Marxism they took the conclusion that Russia had already taken the capitalist path of development and the laws of capitalist development, but dropped the revolutionary content—the development of the contradictions in capitalism, the emergence of the proletariat as the grave-digger of capitalism. The leading representatives of the "legal Marxists" were Peter Struve and Tugan-Baranowsky.—p. 30.

16. This was true of the German and Italian Revolutions of 1848-1849. The abolition of the most antiquated relics of feudalism and the attainment of national unity in Germany and Italy, which were the chief aims of these revolutions, were, in fact, carried out by the Bismarck government in Germany and by Cavour in Italy after the revolutionary movements had been crushed.—p. 32.

17. These reproaches were formulated most fully by Martynov in his *Two Dictatorships* and by Axelrod in his articles in the new *Iskra*. For example, in the article entitled, "The Unity of Russian Social-Democracy and Our Tasks" (*Iskra*, No. 55), Axelrod asserts that the Bolsheviks "merely serve as the representatives of bourgeois ideology in the liberation movement in Russia against absolutism."—p. 35.

18. The "peasant slogans" of the Menshevik Conference are formulated in the resolution, "Work among the Peasants," as follows: "Social-Democrats consider it necessary . . . to agitate for: (a) an open declaration of political demands at village and town meetings; (b) universal arming for the purpose of self-defence against the violence of the government; (c) refusal to pay duties or perform compulsory services; (d) refusal to supply recruits, appear for military training or rally to the colours when reserves are called up; (e) refusal to recognise all government bodies appointed or selected under pressure of the government; (f) the free election of officials—and hence (g) revolutionary local government in the villages and a revolutionary league of village self-governing societies, which are to organise the uprising of the peasants against tsarism."—p. 36*n*.

19. The names are those of a number of liberal papers of various shades, whose political policy Lenin described in 1905 in his article, "The Democratic Tasks of the Revolutionary Proletariat," as follows: "As we all know, an extensive liberal party is rapidly being formed in Russia, to which belong the Emancipation League (*Osvobozhdeniye*) and a large number of Zemstvos, and such newspapers as *Nasha Zhizn* (*Our Life*), *Nashi Dni* (*Our Days*), *Syn Otechestva* (*Son of the Fatherland*), *Russkiye Vedemosti* (*Russian News*), etc. This liberal bourgeois party likes to be known as the Constitutional *Democratic* Party. As a matter of fact, as may be seen from the programme of the illegal *Osvobozhdeniye*, this party is a *monarchist* party. It does not

want a republic. It does not want a single chamber, and in respect of the upper chamber demands indirect and, in effect, non-universal suffrage (residential qualification). It does not by any means desire the transfer of the *whole* of the supreme power of the state to the people although, for the sake of appearances, it loves to talk of the transfer of power to the people! It does not want to *overthrow* the autocracy. All it wants is the division of power among (1) the monarchy, (2) the upper chamber (where the landlords and the capitalist will predominate) and (3) a lower chamber, which *alone* will be constituted on democratic principles."—p. 40.

20. Zemstvos were rural local authorities set up in the sixties after the emancipation of the serfs, and representing exclusively the landowning interests. They appeared at various periods as more or less active, though moderate, opponents of the autocracy. Most of the leaders of the bourgeois political parties which sprang up after October 1905, emerged from and received their political training in the ranks of the Zemstvo.—p. 41.

21. The demand for an upper chamber, to consist solely of representatives of the bourgeoisie, the landlords and the intellectuals, as distinct from a lower chamber elected by universal suffrage, formed an integral part of the programme of the liberal bourgeoisie and the liberal landlords in 1905. The upper chamber was to serve as a check upon the lower chamber, as is the case in England, for example, with the House of Lords, and the Senate in the United States. After 1905, the lower chamber in Russia was represented by the State Duma and the upper chamber by the State Council, which consisted of representatives of the big landlords and government officials.—p. 41.

22. This footnote read as follows: "Of course, we must not allow ourselves to be deceived by the fact that our peasants, as many persons have informed me recently, very readily change from naïve monarchism to an equally naïve republicanism and use arguments to the effect that: the tsar is a fool; he should be kicked out and in the future the tsar should be elected every three years, etc."—41*n*.

23. Father Gapon led the workers' demonstration at the Winter Palace on January 22, 1905 ("Bloody Sunday"), where hundreds were killed and wounded when the troops, on the order of the tsar, fired into the crowd. The movement organised by Gapon was revealed as an attempt to place the labour movement under police control. In January, 1905, Gapon used his organisation (Society of Russian Factory Workers of St. Petersburg) to gain control of the strike movement which began at the Putilov steel works and rapidly spread to all the big factories of the city, affecting some 150,000 workers. Gapon commenced widespread agitation for organising a march to the Winter Palace to deliver a petition to the tsar. On a number of occasions the Bolsheviks spoke at Gapon's meetings against the procession and the petition and issued three leaflets on the eve of January 22 directed against Gapon's scheme. "Bloody Sunday," contrary to the wishes and expectations of its authors, became the starting point of the First Russian Revolution.—p. 44.

24. During the second phase (1792-1793) of the Great French Revolution power was first assumed by the moderate, revolutionary wing of the bourgeoisie, represented by the Girondists, and later by the revolutionary petty-bourgeoisie, represented by the Jacobins. The revolutionary-democratic dictatorship of

the petty bourgeoisie, led by the Jacobins, in the main completed the bourgeois-democratic revolution in France, and did what the big commercial and financial bourgeoisie could not do and what the moderate revolutionary wing of the bourgeoisie did not dare to do.—p. 47.

25. These were the various names by which the Bolsheviks were known in 1905: *Vperyod*-ists, from the Bolshevik paper *Vperyod* (*Forward*), which appeared in Geneva from about the end of 1904 to the time of the Third Party Congress; Congress-ists, as distinct from the Mensheviks, who were followers of the Geneva Conference; *Proletary*-ists, from *Proletary*, which was the central organ of the Party after the Third Congress.—p. 48.

26. According to the Mensheviks the placing of formal demands and conditions for the support of the Liberals by the proletarian party plays a rôle with regard to politics similar to litmus paper, which is used to test chemical solutions for acidity. At the Second Congress (1903) Starover (A. N. Potressov), in opposition to the resolution of Plekhanov and Lenin on the position to be taken with regard to the Liberals, proposed another resolution enumerating the conditions for an understanding with the Liberals. These conditions were to serve as political *litmus paper,* for the opportunity would be accorded for testing the reaction of the Liberals. In connection with one of such attempts of the Mensheviks to put formal conditions to the Liberals, Lenin remarked: "Philistine, write out your promissory note!"—p. 52.

27. "Parliamentary cretinism" is an expression repeatedly used by Marx and Engels in their historical works. Thus Marx in his *Eighteenth Brumaire* talks of "parliamentary cretinism" as "a peculiar disease which was raging on the entire Continent in 1848." Engels in his *Germany: Revolution and Counter-Revolution* describes the democrats in the Frankfort parliament as being "sick with an incurable disease of *parliamentary cretinism,* an illness which makes its unhappy victims suffer from a lofty illusion that the whole world, its history and its future, are directed and predestined by a majority in a given representative institution, which they honour with their membership."—p. 52.

28. Differences of opinion on the agrarian question arose between Kautsky and Bebel at the Congress of the German Social-Democracy at Breslau, October 1895. Here an overwhelming majority of votes was cast in favor of a resolution proposed by Kautsky, Clara Zetkin and others which rejected the resolution supported by Bebel as opportunistic.—p. 54*n.*

29. Demagogic appeals by the opportunist wing of the Russian Social-Democratic Labour Party for an immediate attack were made in the Spring of 1901 at the very height of the demonstration movement. One of the leaflets called upon the workers to "Form a storming line!" Appeals for an immediate attack were also made by Nadezhdin in his pamphlet, *The Eve of the Revolution.* The quotation about the economic struggle is from the resolution of the Fourth Congress of the Bund.—p. 58.

30. The reference is to the following passage in Engels' article, "The Programme of the Blanquist Communards": "During every revolution many stupid things are done just as at any other time, and when people have at last cooled down sufficiently to adopt a critical attitude towards events they

are bound to come to the following conclusion: we did many things that would have been better left undone, and left undone much that should have been done, and that is why things went wrong.

"What a lack of criticism is displayed by those who positively make an idol of the Commune and regard it as infallible, declaring that every building it set fire to deserved to be burnt down and that every hostage it shot deserved to be shot! Is that not equivalent to declaring that during the May Week the people shot exactly those individuals who should have been shot, and no others; that only such buildings were burnt down as should have been burnt down, and no others? Is that not equivalent to asserting, as was asserted of the first French Revolution, that every individual who was executed in the course of that revolution deserved his fate—from those whom Robespierre executed, to Robespierre himself? To such depths of folly can individuals descend who are really absolutely innocuous, but want themselves at all costs to be regarded as terrible."—p. 67.

31. Lenin does not give here a complete appraisal of the Paris Commune, to which he attributed the greatest importance and the history of which he profoundly studied. Of the services it performed he wrote on another occasion as follows: "But with all its errors, the Commune is the greatest example of the greatest proletarian movement of the nineteenth century. Marx valued very highly the historical importance of the Commune: if, during the treacherous raid of the Versailles gang on the arms of the Paris proletariat, the workers had given them up without a fight, the disastrous effect of the demoralisation which such weakness would have brought into the proletarian movement would have been much more serious than the injury from the losses suffered by the working class in the fight while defending its arms. Great as were the sacrifices of the Commune, they are redeemed by its importance for the general proletarian struggle: it stirred up the socialist movement throughout Europe, it demonstrated the value of civil war, it dispersed patriotic illusions and shattered the naïve faith in the common national aspirations of the bourgeoisie. The Commune has taught the European proletariat to deal concretely with the problems of the socialist revolution." (V. I. Lenin, *The Paris Commune*, Little Lenin Library, p. 19.)—p. 68.

32. The Erfurt Programme is the programme of the Social-Democratic Party of Germany adopted at its Congress in Erfurt, 1891. The programme was drafted and edited by Karl Kautsky. Engels' comments on the draft programme to which Lenin refers, were made in a letter to Kautsky dated June 29, 1891, but published only in 1901, in *Die Neue Zeit*, the theoretical organ of the Social-Democratic Party, under the heading, *A Contribution to the Criticism of the Draft Social-Democratic Programme*. Lenin dealt in detail with Engels' letter in his *State and Revolution* and attached considerable importance to it as "criticism . . ." of ". . . the *opportunist* views of Social-Democracy regarding question of *state* organisation." (Lenin's italics.) ". . . And when we remember," says Lenin in this book, "what importance the Erfurt Programme has acquired in international Social-Democracy, how it has become the model for the whole of the Second International, it may, without exaggeration, be said that Engels thereby criticised the opportunism of the whole Second International." (*Collected Works*, Vol. XXI, Book II, pp. 203, 204; also *Little Lenin Library*, Vol. 14.)

In the present instance, Lenin refers to Engels' reference to the importance of the democratic republic for the struggle of the proletariat for its dictatorship when he said: "Now, it seems not to be feasible legally to put the demand for a republic into the programme, although that was as possible even under Louis Philippe in France as in Italy today. But the fact that one cannot even draw up an openly republican party programme in Germany proves how colossal is the illusion that the republic can be established in an amiable, peaceful fashion, and not only the republic but communist society as well. None the less, it is possible, if need be, to squeeze by the republic. But what must and can be put in, in my opinion, is the demand for the *concentration of all political power in the hands of the people's representatives.* And that would be sufficient for the present, if one cannot go any further."—p. 72.

33. Engels' letter to Turati, dated January 26, 1894, was published in 1895, soon after Engels' death, in No. 3 of *Critica Sociale,* Milan. The letter was written in connection with the discussion which went on within the Italian Socialist Party on the so-called "hunger riot" of the peasants in Sicily. It contained a general estimate of the internal situation in Italy and also the author's view on the character of the approaching revolution and the tactics which the revolutionary Marxian party ought to pursue. The letter is included in *The Correspondence of Marx and Engels* (International Publishers), pp. 519-525.—p. 73.

34. The reference is to the followers of the Russian anarchist leader, Michael Bakunin, who were expelled from the International Workingmen's Association, and to the resolution issued by the Bakuninists in opposition to participation in a provisional revolutionary government in September 1872. The first Spanish Revolution, establishing a republic, began in February 1873. Engels refers to the Bakuninist resolution in his article, "Bakuninists at Work," published in the *Volksstadt,* organ of the German Social-Democracy, in 1873. Lenin wrote on the same question in May 1905, in his article, "On the Provisional Revolutionary Government." (*Collected Works,* Vol. VII.)—p. 79.

35. *Credo* was the name applied to a document in which the views of the Economists were proclaimed for the first time. Under the leadership of Lenin, who was then in exile in Siberia, and at his instance, a group of exiles protested against this document, and this protest became of great importance for the future history of the Party. The *Credo* and the protest against it are given in Lenin's *Selected Works,* Vol. II.—p. 81.

36. Lenin here refers to the controversy between Kautsky and Bernstein at the end of the nineties of the last century. Replying to Bernstein's assertion that Social-Democracy is prematurely striving for political power and that it should remain an opposition party for an indefinitely long period, Kautsky, in his book *Anti-Bernstein,* puts the question: "Dare we win?" And he replies: "The party that wants to exist must fight, and to fight means trying to win. And those who try to win must always reckon with the possibility that they will be the victors. If we want to guarantee ourselves against power falling into our hands prematurely, the only thing we can do is to go to sleep." Nevertheless, in this very book, Kautsky depicts the victory of the Party, its accession to power, in an *opportunist manner.* He depicts it, not as the violent overthrow of the bourgeoisie, but as a peaceful victory at the polls. On this point also, as on the fundamental question of the revolution, *i.e.,* the dictatorship of the proletariat, Kautsky in his polemics with Bernstein "surrenders the position to opportunism."—p. 91.

37. This refers to Kautsky's article, "The Split in Russian Social-Democracy," published in the new (Menshevik) *Iskra* of June 28 (15), 1905. Even before this period, in the period between the Second and Third Congress of the R.S.-D.L.P., Kautsky, like all the centrist leaders of the Social-Democratic Party of Germany and of the Second International, supported the Mensheviks against Lenin and the Bolsheviks on the question of the split. In the article mentioned, Kautsky pursues the same anti-Bolshevik line, and on the main theoretical point of difference between the Bolsheviks and the Mensheviks, *viz.*, the provisional revolutionary government, he writes the following: ". . . A foreign observer must exert great effort to discover any difference between the two factions. The principal question that divides them at the present time is, whether or not members of the Party should take part in the future revolutionary government. But surely, it is possible to discuss how the skin of the bear that has not been killed yet is to be divided in a peaceful manner within a single party; moreover, the whole controversy is futile as long as absolutely nothing is known of what the revolutionary government in which we are to take part will look like."—p. 92.